ISBN 978-0-483-59503-3
PIBN 10790505

THE COLE LECTURES.

Col. E. W. Cole, of Nashville, Tenn., has given in trust to the Bishops of the Methodist Episcopal Church, South, the sum of two thousand five hundred dollars, the design and conditions of which bequest are stated as follows:

"The object of this fund is to establish a foundation for a perpetual lectureship in connection with the Biblical Department of the University, to be restricted in its scope to a defense and advocacy of the Christian Religion. These lectures shall be delivered at such intervals, from time to time, as shall be deemed best; and the particular theme and lecturer shall be determined by nomination of the Theological Faculty and confirmation of the College of Bishops of the Methodist Episcopal Church, South. Said lectures shall always be reduced to writing in full, and the manuscript of the same shall be the property of the University, to be published or otherwise disposed of by the Board of Trust at its discretion, the net proceeds arising therefrom to be added to the foundation fund or otherwise used for the benefit of the Biblical Department."

THE WITNESSES TO CHRIST,

THE SAVIOUR OF THE WORLD.

—

LECTURES

DELIVERED BEFORE THE BIBLICAL DEPARTMENT OF VANDERBILT UNIVERSITY.

—

BY ALPHEUS W. WILSON, D.D.,

One of the Bishops of the Methodist Episcopal Church, South.

—

NASHVILLE, TENN.:
PUBLISHING HOUSE OF THE M. E. CHURCH, SOUTH.
BARBEE & SMITH, AGENTS.
1894.

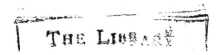

PREFACE.

IT was with great reluctance that the work of preparing and delivering these lectures was undertaken. The habits of a lifetime are not easily set aside; and the mental characteristics fixed by long and exclusive practice in extempore preaching do not readily adjust themselves to the demand for written sermons. The desk is an insufficient substitute for the presence of the living congregation, and offers no stimulus to a sluggish brain. The pen becomes an unwieldy instrument under these conditions, and the fruit of such labor is apt to be vanity and vexation of spirit. Only the feeling that refusal would be ungracious and the hope that this first course of the "Cole Lectures" might somehow serve as a note of direction for better and abler successors in this field induced the acceptance of the call.

The purpose of this series is simple and single. It is intended to set forth the claims of our divine Lord as resting upon a basis of facts belonging to the region of eternal things and requiring for their establishment testimony from the same sphere. The evidences of Christianity on the historical and merely intellectual side have no place in the statement, not because their value is not appreciated, but for the reasons given in the lectures: that they can only touch the earthly and human side of the revelation, do not include the ultimate facts, and can never finally and fully satisfy the conscience and heart of the world.

The defects of the statement are many. They result in part from the considerations above given, in part from the necessity of keeping within prescribed limits, and partly from the unavoidable haste of the work.

Such as they are, they go forth with the hope and prayer that they may help to a better and truer faith in the Son of the living God and contribute in some small measure, however remotely, to that which was the dearest purpose and controlling aim of his incarnate life: the salvation of men.

A. W. W

May 24, 1894.

SYNOPSIS.

—

LECTURE I.

THE INADEQUACY OF HUMAN TESTIMONY.

PAGES

Treatment of Questions Concerning His Person........ 3

Not Dogmatic. Facts................................. 4

Certainty Demanded and Provided.................... 5, 6

His Own Statement.................................. 6–8

Value and Order of It.............................. 9, 10

Testimony of John the Baptist...................... 10–12

Valid, not Final. Facts not within Human Observation. 13, 14

Not Capable of Being Conceived by the Wisdom of this
    World. Its Faiths and Philosophy................ 14–17

Insufficiency of Science........................... 18–21

Results of Mere Human Testimony in Skepticism and
    Uncertainty................................... 21–23

Illustrations from Gospels......................... 23, 24

Now and Then...................................... 24, 25

His Own Disciples................................. 26–30

Practical Value of Human Testimony................. 31

Applied to the Historical Side of the Gospel....... 31, 32

Transcendent Character of the Gospel............... 32–34

Apostolic Appeal.................................. 35, 36

The Peril and the Need of To-day.................. 37–40

LECTURE II.

THE CONJOINT TESTIMONY OF THE FATHER AND THE SON.

Witness of Angels Excluded......................... 43–46

Necessity for Divine Testimony..................... 46–48

Natural Ways of Divine Manifestation............... 48–50

Highest and Final Form of Revelation: Father and Son. 50–52

(vii)

                                                               PAGES
Insufficiency of Deistic or Unitarian Conception of God. 52–54

God, Father. Father, Son. Trinity.................. 54–56

Conjoint Testimony, Confirming Ancient Monotheistic
    Teaching 56–58

Transcendent Statement of the Gospel................ 58–60

Ethnic Conceptions of God. Ethical Failure.......... 61, 62

Philosophic and Scientific Notions; Moral and Spiritual
    Degeneracy and Loss of Hope..................... 62–65

Ground of Testimony of the Gospel; Possible Direct In-
    tercourse between God and Man................... 66, 67

Spiritual Faculty in Man........................... 67–70

Ethical Quality Divine. Righteousness, Law, Con-
    science 70–75

Love; Equally Disclosure of God in Relations of Father
    and Son.. 75, 76

Conjunction of Righteousness and Love the Complete
    Revelation of Father and Son 76–78

Special Articulate Utterance at Baptism and Transfigu-
    ration Culmination of Testimonies................. 78–81

Summary 82, 83

LECTURE III.
THE TESTIMONY OF THE WORKS.

Identity in Working of Father and Son............ .... 87, 88

The Works Natural Expressions of the Son........... 88

Work and Works; a Single Purpose 88

Only Such as the Father Gave Him to Do.............. 89, 90

Completion of Work of the Father.................... 90

Purpose, Salvation of Men 91

His Work: 1. Revelation of God 91–93

    Natural and Hebraic Revelations............... 93, 94

    Our Lord's Advance upon These............... . 95

    Knowledge of God Determined by Relation to the
        Son... 95–97

PAGES

2. Revelation of Man...................................... 97

(1) Communion with God, Which Is Essential to
the Knowledge of God, Affirms Possible
Worth and Power of Human Nature....... 97, 98

Illustrated in Son of Man................... 98, 99

(2) By This the Ethical Relations of Man Are
Determined.............................. 99

By Reaffirmation of Righteous Relations between God and Man.................... 99, 100

By Referring These Relations to Their Source
in the Godhead......................... 100, 101

3. His Work Redemptive....................... 101–103

(1) By Completing the Revelation of Sin........ 103

Use, Limitations, and Enlargement of Law... 103–106

Standard of Righteousness in Jesus Christ.... 106–108

(2) By Remission of Sins.... 108–110

Exclusive Authority of Jesus Christ........ 110

Referred to His Eternal Relations with God
and Consequent Relations with the World. 110–116

His Entrance into Human History; Assertion
of His Authority and Rights.............. 116–119

Oneness of the Race................... ... 120, 121

Identification with the Body of Humanity..... 121

Nature of His Redemptive Work Suggested:

1. By His Relations to the World as Head........ 122

2. By His Relations from the Human Side to God. 123

3. By His Fulfillment of All Righteousness....... 123

4. By His Endurance of Human Penalty.......... 123

5. By His Vindication in the Resurrection........ 123

His Works: As Signs. 124, 125

As Assertions of His Authority................... 125, 126

Attestations of the Divinity of His Person......... 126, 127

Expressions of the Mind of God toward Man...... 127

LECTURE IV.

The Witness of the Scriptures.

PAGES

Appeal to the Scriptures.................... .... 131, 132
  1. The Old Testament and the New Stand or Fall
     Together......... 132
  2. The Old Testament Intended for the "Ages to
     Come.".........................·................... 133, 134
  3. The Scriptures Were Inspired of God......... 134, 135
     To Be Read by the Light of Later Times........ 135, 136
     The Right Reading of Them................... 136, 137
     Preparatory.................................... 137, 138
     Preparation in Gentile History................ 138, 139
     Prophetic Element............................ 140–142
     The Promise................................... 142–144
     The Covenant................................. 144–146
     Special Manifestations of God................. 146–148
     Progress of Revelation........................ 148–151
     Pre-Mosaic Standard of Righteousness and Di-
        vine Discipline............................. 151–155
     Place and Function of the Law................ 155–157
     Its Religious and Its Secular Side............., 157
     Priesthood.................................... 157, 158
     Sacrifice...................................... 158, 159
     Ceremonial System........................... 159
     Civil Polity................................... 159, 160
     Insufficiency of the Law..................... 161–163
Prophecy: Its Institution, Functions, and Growth..... 163–167
  Its Fulfillment................................... 168, 169

LECTURE V.

The Testimony of the Spirit.

The Comforter Christ's Final Provision for His Church. 173–174
Complement and Completion of All Antecedent Reve-
  ·lation 174–176

His Place in the Life of the Son of Man.............. 176, 177

1. His Name: "Comforter"...................... 177, 178
2. Sent by the Son.............................. 178
3. Sent from the Father......................... 179
4. Spirit of Truth............................ 179, 180
5. He Testifies of Christ...................... 180, 181

His Testimony to Chosen Disciples................. 181–183

By Personal Communion......................... 184–187

With Individuals; not Body Corporate........... 187, 188

He "Opened Their Understanding"............... 188–192

First Outward Effect of His Coming Was upon
Speech.................................. 192

Gift of Power................................. 192, 193

Completeness of His Operation.................. 194

Its Typical Character; and Distinct from Outward
and Sensuous Service...................... 195, 196

Source and Test of Character and Director of all
Christian Activities........................ 196–199

Estimate of the Gift as Compared with the Incarnate Life........ 199–201

His Testimony to the World....................... 201, 202

In Conviction of Sin........................... 202–205

In Conviction of Righteousness................. 205–207

In Conviction of Judgment...................... 207–208

He Bears Witness through Human Agency.......... 209, 210

The Sum of It All............................... 210, 211

LECTURE VI.

The Testimony of the Church.

Résumé of Facts................................ 215

Résumé of Proofs............................... 216

Completed Testimony:

Committed, on Divine Side, to the Holy Spirit. ... 216, 217

On Human Side, to Man "Chosen before of God".. 217, 218

PAGES

Value of Human Element......................... 218, 219

Witnesses Must Have Immediate Knowledge...... 219–222

Witnesses to Be Vindicated. Demonstration of the

    Spirit... 222, 223

Gifts of Power and Its Effect.................... 223, 224

Power of the Spirit, Its Nature and Operation...... 224, 225

Character of the Church......................... 225–227

Competency of Witnesses......................... 227–229

Form of Testimony of the Church.................. 229

   1. It Reproduces Ideal of the Lord's Life and Work   229

    In Personal Experience, Conformity to the Im-

      age of the Son of God..................... 229–234

    Methods of Life and Growth.................. 234–236

    Power and Completeness of Individual Life..... 236, 237

   2. It Secures and Conveys the Testimony.......... 237

    As Having in Custody the Oracles of God....... 237

    As Recording the Lord's Life and Its Conse-

      quents..................................... 237, 238

    As Guarding the Course and Text of Scripture.. 238–240

    It Provides the Evidences, Historical and Crit-

      ical, of Christianity......................... 240, 241

   3. It Bears Its Witness in the Order and Adminis-

      tration of the Church....................... 241, 242

    Discipline.................................... 242

    Public Worship and Sacraments................ 242, 243

    Organized Agencies for Doing Good............ 244

   4. Relations of Church to Secular Life............ 245, 246

Conclusion... 247, 248

LECTURE I.

THE INADEQUACY OF HUMAN TESTIMONY.

(1)

"Ye sent unto John, and he bare witness unto the truth. But I receive not testimony from man: but these things I say, that ye might be saved." John v. 33, 34.

THE questions that were raised concerning himself, whatever might have been the motive that prompted them, were not treated by our Lord in a speculative way, or to satisfy the demand of the intellect. His point of view and line of statement were thoroughly and exclusively practical. According to his avowed purpose, his speech and his life were directed upon the one end of human salvation. "These things I say, that ye might be saved." It was inevitable that the truths he uttered and the claims he made should provoke discussion. There is no authority so high that it will suffice to still the curious questionings of men. But it was not as matter for dialectics that he advanced his claim and declared the truth of his person. According to his view, the world needed to know him in order to be saved. "If ye believe not that I am he, ye shall die in your sins."

(3)

It follows that the question is not to be treated
in a merely dogmatic way. It has become so
much the habit of theology to treat the person of
Christ as a matter of doctrinal statement and definitions that its character and value as a fact have
been obscured. Who was he? what was he? not
how, were the questions to which he gave answer,
and in settlement of which he appealed to the appropriate testimonies. He gave no explanations
and entered upon no defense of the mysteries involved in his claims. He knew, as we know, that
the nearer we come to God and the truer and
more distinct our consciousness of him, the more
impossible it becomes to define and explain him,
and the more impotent and unappreciable is any
defense of his nature and claims set up before the
mere human understanding. "With the heart
man believeth." The fact enters into the experi-
rience of countless multitudes who know God,
while they are wholly incompetent to pursue the
cold calculations of the intellect which, far as they
reach and vast as is their compass, have not found
out God.

In truth, the issues involved were too great both
as effecting his own rightful place in the universe,
and as touching the destinies of the world, to be
committed to the uncertainties of doctrinal discus-

sion. He spake as one having authority, and proposed to satisfy the demand of his Church and of the individual conscience with nothing less than the certainty of those things wherein they were instructed. Doubtful disputations concerning even minor matters are of doubtful utility; but when they touch the very substance of our gospel and reduce the person of the Son of God to the level of a thesis for intellectual discussion we feel that the sanctities of the Godhead are invaded, the temple of the Father desecrated, and the dearest and most sacred experiences of the Christian soul tossed to and fro as the sport and plaything of a profane curiosity. No dishonoring uncertainty has characterized the confession of the Church of God from the days of the apostles to the present. Through storm and tumult and change, in the face of skepticism and despite opposition, with unfaltering utterance she has reiterated the great facts: "I believe in God, the Father Almighty, Maker of heaven and earth, and in Jesus Christ, his only begotten Son, our Lord." With invincible conviction she has proclaimed these facts as the only ground of hope for the world and the center of attraction for all worlds, indispensable to the order and harmony of the universe. For in him are to be gathered together under one head all things which are in heaven and which are on earth. Uncertainty and doubt are fatal to the mission of the Church.

Jesus Christ did not fail to make ample provision for the confirmation and full assurance of faith. The testimony which he adduces should be preceded by a summary account of his character and claims as given by himself and attested by the witnesses to which he appeals.

The name which was divinely given him before his birth, Jesus, includes, when searched by the light of its purpose and of his own teaching and work, all that is expressed in names and titles afterward assumed or given, and finds its only sufficient explanation in them. His name shall be called Jesus—Saviour—because " he shall save his people from their sins," for his power to do this involves his own freedom from and absolute superiority to all sin, his right to control the lives and hearts of men, and divine authority to do away with sin by forgiveness through the sacrifice of himself. He has the name, not in virtue of his work as the messenger of God's offer of forgiveness, but because of his own person and the rights and powers inseparable therefrom. The " Son of Man," his most frequent appellation, distinguishes him from all men, and asserts for him an ideal character and representative relation involving the interests of the race. The "Christ," the "Anointed," puts him in the place claimed for the Messiah of the Old Testament, while the pregnant phrase so often joined to it, "Son of the Living God," lifts him above the plane of Jewish thought of the Messiah, and refers the Messianic character to his immediate relationship in nature and being to the interior life of the invisible God.   When to these are added his oft-repeated declarations concerning his relations with the Godhead, such as " The Father sent me "—not sent from any point or condition of finite life, but from God, from the inner life of the Godhead, from the " bosom of the Father " into the life of the world, or even more intensely spoken, " I proceeded forth and came from God; " " Not that any man hath seen the Father, save he which is of God, he hath seen the Father;" " No man hath ascended up to heaven, but he that came down from heaven;" "He that hath seen me hath seen the Father;" "I and my Father are one;" "That all men should honor the Son, even as they honor the Father," and many other direct and incidental assertions of prerogative and power essential to his character, there is found ample vindication of the whole breadth and depth of New Testament teach-

ing, and of the faith of the true Church of God
through all its ages.   He is God "manifest in the
flesh;" "the Son—the brightness of the glory of
the Father, and the express image of his person,
who when he had by himself purged our sins, sat
down on the right hand of the Majesty on high,"
"the image of the invisible God, the firstborn of
every creature [of all creation]."   The complete
statement is given in the prologue, as it is called,
the true beginning, the thesis of the Gospel of
John, a summary of the facts concerning his person, upon which all the testimonies are brought to
bear and all hope for men depends.   "In the beginning was the Word, and the Word was with
God, and the Word was God.   The same was in
the beginning with God.   All things were made
by him; and without him was not anything made
that was made.   In him was life; and the life was
the light of men.   .   .   .   That was the true light,
which lighteth every man that cometh into the
world.   .   .   .   And the Word was made flesh,
and dwelt among us, (and we beheld his glory, the
glory as of the only begotten of the Father,) full
of grace and truth."

We are constrained to take these statements of
himself as the starting point of our inquiry.   For
first the testimonies which we shall consider are to

be estimated according to their appropriateness to this view. Further, his entire life of speech, work, and suffering was conformed to those statements and must find in them its sufficient account and its full explanation. Besides, the very existence, perpetuity, and success of the Church as his witness and representative in the world are conditioned upon the sufficiency and truthfulness of his own declarations; and the whole body of New Testament teaching concerning his person and work is but the expansion of, and must be vindicated by his utterances, else your faith is vain. Here, as in its first application, is his saying true: "The word that I have spoken, that shall judge you." At the very outset we ask, as did the Jews, "Whom makest thou thyself?"

The answer which he furnishes is distinct and unequivocal. It is true that there was in his earlier ministry a measure of reserve and even reticence that contrasts strongly with his later—especially his Judean—teachings. That was to be expected. It is agreement with divine methods of dealing with men. He taught as they were able to bear it. There was no uncertainty, no ambiguity in his life and relations to the world. From the first he assumed the position of rightful superiority to, and authority over all men—Moses and the prophets included—that was without precedent or parallel. The sermon on the Mount is as significant and emphatic in the assertion of this preëminence, as the later chapters of John's Gospel. Beginning with such an assumption, by gradual disclosures in life and teaching he opened the understanding of his disciples until they were prepared for the great revelation—which at the time seemed to them final, the fullest that could be made—issuing in the great confession: "Thou art the Christ, the Son of the living God." But "from that time," the moment of Peter's exultant acknowledgment, he taught them in other form, and out of the deepening gloom of his humiliation gave intenser and more distinct impression to his consciousness of divine sonship. As the antagonisms of the world became fiercer and its hate more malignant, his assertion of himself became more pronounced and his offer of himself to the faith and hope of men more earnest as well as more significant. He used all legitimate means for securing conviction, and in this behalf appealed to all available witnesses.

In the order of narrative John the Baptist appears as the first witness to the truth. His descent, character, and life were his credentials. Born into a priestly line, he was entitled to the place and prerogative attaching to his hereditary calling. The circumstances of his birth signalized him as set apart for an entraordinary mission to the chosen people. His early home training was under the direction of parents who "were both righteous before God, walking in all the commandments and ordinances of the Lord blameless." Years of solitude and meditation in the wilderness, far from the stir and passion and artificial conditions of city life, contributed to his self-discipline and the integrity of his character, attested by his complete renunciation of all things not necessary to the fulfillment of his course. With all these, his prophetic standing and his fearless utterance secured for him a commanding position among the people and gave authority to his testimony. He occupied the highest place in public estimation; and people of all classes, including scribes and Pharisees, came to his baptism. When the Jews of Jerusalem sent to him priests and Levites to inquire into his claims, he made distinct and unambiguous answer: "I am not the Christ. I am the voice of one crying in the wilderness, make straight the way of the Lord, as said the prophet Esais. There standeth one among you whom ye know not. He it is who coming after me is preferred before me, whose shoe's latchet I am not worthy to unloose." As reported in the synoptic Gospels, "He shall baptize you with the Holy Ghost, and with fire." A little later he points to Jesus as " the Lamb of God that taketh away the sin of the world," and with increasing urgency he bare record saying, " I saw the Spirit descending from heaven like a dove, and it abode upon him. And I knew him not; but he that sent me to baptize with water, the same said unto me, Upon whom thou shalt see the Spirit descending and remaining on him, the same is he which baptizeth with the Holy Ghost. And I saw, and bare record that this is the Son of God." More direct and decisive testimony could have been given by no man. Nor is its force abated by the fact that in the last days of his life, when he knew that his work was done, he sent from his prison messengers to Jesus saying: "Art thou he that should come, or do we look for another?" Such a question could have had no meaning addressed to one of whom he stood in doubt. It was, indeed, his final official act transferring his work and his disciples to the Master to whom he had testified. Conforming himself to the divine method of life and teaching, he would have them put their faith not in his testimony, but in what they should see and hear from the Lord himself.

Jesus certainly did not intend to repudiate such

testimony. He certifies its validity by his own words: "Ye sent unto John and he bare witness to the truth." It had inestimable value as a prophetic announcement of his entrance upon his great work, and was in perfect agreement with the whole body of prophetic scriptures to which he afterward appealed. It was the indispensable preparation for his ministry. It is yet more evident that he did not intend to exclude such witness, seeing that in arranging for the propagation of the gospel he commissioned men whose supreme, almost exclusive function was to testify of him. The nature and value of their testimony will be considered hereafter. It is enough here to note the fact that we may put a true construction upon his words, " I receive not testimony from man." He does not intend that the validity of his claim shall finally depend upon the sufficiency of any human testimony. In the terms of St. Paul when disclaiming the right of dominion over the faith of the Church, " Your faith should not stand in the wisdom of men."

The substance of the gospel—that is to say, all that is involved in the person, the power, and coming of our Lord Jesus Christ—lies beyond the possible range of human observation and investigation. It is indissolubly linked to an antecedent life—" before the foundation of the world "—quite as essential to the work he was sent to do, and to the sufficiency of the sacrificial offering of himself, as the manifested life in the flesh, and to a subsequent life of princely station and saving power in most intimate relation to the Church in its militant state and vital to its final triumph and reward.   Indeed, whatever value we may attach to the life, labors, and sufferings of Jesus of Nazareth, viewed as an incident, or an episode in the course of human history, it is impossible to exalt them to the supreme place of the saving power for the world, and set him as the bearer of the sin of the world, unless we can lift him above the plane of mere human action and endurance, and concede to him command of the ultimate sources of wisdom and power.   For the whole tendency of human character, and all the energies of human will in the individual and in the race, from the beginning of time—to say nothing of preternatural solicitation and influence—are expressed in the term sin; and to take away sin the tendency must be reversed and the will controlled and directed by forces mightier than human passion and endeavor, and more subtle than the finest and most secret instincts of the race.

The conception of such a life and its entrance into our state was foreign to the wisdom of this world, whether expressed in the false faiths that have grown out of the sense of evil dominant in nature and the dread of worse to come, or out of the striving of the few better souls after the knowledge of God, or in the philosophies which exhausted the resources of intellect in the effort to find the ground of being and define the relations between God and the world.   Ample proof and illustration of this may be found in the painful and futile strivings, continued to our own day, of Oriental worshipers to rid themselves of the embarrassment and oppression of sin, and find some way of bringing God and man together. Their notions of God were almost entirely void of ethical contents, and issued in blurred and confused conceptions of sin.   For the most part they could not separate the idea of evil from finite existence, and hoped for release only in the ultimate absorption of all being in God.   Thus the conscience of sin disappeared from among them; while, on the other hand, their view of God was resolved into polytheistic theories, and their avatars were reduced to unreal appearances.   Their abstruse philosophies, as far removed from the true order and practical issues of intellectual life as their faith and worship were from the demand and hope of the ethical and spiritual life, left them without any ba-

sis in thought for the distinction between God and
the world, and rendered a reconciliation between
them impossible.   In form or in tendency they were
atheistic, agnostic, pantheistic, or polytheistic; or
rather it might be said that all these forms and tendencies, driven by the irrepressible needs of human nature, issued in a gross polytheism—"gods
many and lord's many."   The dualism of Zoroas-
ter and the naturalistic worship of the Egyptians,
and even their "esoteric" doctrines, speculative
rather than practical, form no exception.   They
are equally far removed from the Christian view
of God and man, their real distinction and intimate
relation with each other, of the sin of the world
and the saving power and process set forth in the
incarnation.   In this view the gospel is absolutely
unique.   The life which was the light of men appears only in its provision.   It unmeasurably transcends even the old Hebrew thought, and, appealing to the law and the prophets as witnesses to its
Christ, presents him in such radiance of divine
glory and fullness of divine life that even the children of the prophets are startled and amazed,
while reverent prophetic souls like Isaiah abase
themselves with humble confession before the
throne and worship.   It is the marvel of the gospel that in the person of the God-man, the "Word

made flesh," it incorporates the Godhead into the body of our humanity, without abasing one jot or tittle of the reverence due to the king, eternal, immortal, invisible, or lessening the sense of sin in the conscience. Rather by the assumption of the "likeness of sinful flesh" sin is made exceeding sinful and worship more true, profound, and spiritual. It was the ethical failure of the heathen religions that made impossible to them the idea of a true union of God and man, and led, on the one side, to the view so often expressed among them of a temporary transformation, apparent rather than real, of their gods into the likeness of men, and the final extinction of the finite by absorption into the divine; and on the other, to the exaltation of man to the state of the gods, the apotheosis of our nature, yet dominated by the resistless power of fate, to which even the will of the supreme gods was subject.

Nowhere outside of Christian life and thought has the idea of the true and permanent conjunction and coëxistence of God and man in one personality been considered. "The world by wisdom knew not God;" and failing to discern him, it was hopelessly ignorant of the spiritual and ethical elements needed to mediate between God and man, and to lay the ground for redemption to right-

2

eousness in a true and complete incarnation. In all the course of its researches and efforts it has given illustration of the prophetic statement as quoted by the apostle, "Eye hath not seen, nor ear heard, neither have entered into the heart of man, the things which God hath prepared for them that love him." As by no method of worship and by no processes of philosophy the truth of the gospel could be attained, so neither could it be discovered by any direct personal observation or investigation. The natural man has no faculties by which he may bridge the mighty chasm between the seen and the unseen, or project himself beyond the boundaries of actual experience and bring within the scope of his knowledge the facts and forces belonging to the world that lies outside the region of sensible observation. The natural faculties may be mightily aided and enlarged in their sphere by the appliances and methods discovered and invented with the increase of knowledge. By these helps the area of accepted facts and conclusions has been so far extended that some minds have determined that there can be nothing which is not reducible to the terms of materialism; or that, if there be aught beyond, it cannot be known. It is true that the limit fixed by the systems of the past are daily pushed farther out, and spaces, worlds, and forces are included in the order of our day that were not dreamed of in the imaginings of the generations gone. But there is a limit nevertheless. Physical science, by the very terms of its existence, as well as by the conditions under which it does its work, is forever confined to matter and force. Whatever does not come under these categories can never be subjected to its processes. Deceived by the close connections of mind and matter, and determined to find within its own sphere account of the strange phenomena resulting from and depending upon these connections, it attempts to resolve the subtle, indefinable, spiritual elements of human nature and life into forms of force and denies to them any higher or other place than it assigns to the dynamics of the material universe. The failure—as in the persistent effort to find the sources and meaning of life—but emphasizes the limitations of research and warns the bold investigator back within his own lines. Still more certainly does the closest and most diligent inquiry find itself baffled and defeated when it attempts to pass beyond the boundaries of time and space and uncover the mysteries of the eternal state and bring into view the facts of the divine life. The immediate and inevitable result of such endeavor has been to substitute conjecture for fact

and speculation for the process of true scientific
research.   If the person and work of our Lord be
held as veritable facts with the momentous issues
of human history and final destiny depending upon
them, they cannot be left to the uncertainties of
such methods. ·The ruling power of this world
and all worlds cannot be treated as a conjecture,
nor the tremendous concerns of eternity suspended.
upon the validity and sufficiency of a speculation
and a theory.   The best results of any hypothesis
—call it a " working hypothesis," if you wish to
assert for it a possible value—with deductions, inferences, and conclusions, can rest upon nothing
more than human authority.   To insure certainty
for them, an infallible reason must be predicated
and absolutely perfect instruments and methods of
inquiry.   It has not yet come into the range of human experience that such conditions have been
provided, save in the single case of Him who is the
subject of investigation, and him the world did not
believe. The long catalogue of difficulties en-
countered and errors exposed in every line of research led a diligent student, himself eminent in
science, to ask: " How can we be sure that there
may not be still other causes of constant error in-
validating our results?" His own answer is:
" Obviously we cannot be sure."   He trusts to the

future to revise results and correct mistakes, and has hope that through slow and halting progress the truth will finally be reached. But, taking counsel of experience, and seeing that with every advance of knowledge the problems of life become more complicated and difficult of solution, will we, can we ever be sure that errors have been avoided, or content ourselves with results as final and satisfactory, save in the comparatively few cases where material things are concerned and exhaustive experiment can verify the work, or mathematics establish the conclusion with the certainty of an infallible calculation?

If we are to be restricted to mere human testimony, we shall be constrained to accept the skeptical position and admit that there is no warrant in experience for the wonders of the gospel, and that no amount of testimony is sufficient to overcome the weight of experience against them. The change of attitude, so often observed, in offering apology for the miracle instead of relying upon it in proof of our Lord's claim, and the shifts and evasions resorted to in order to get rid of it, or reduce it to the plane of a natural and normal event, or incident, show how firmly the conviction of the fallibility and insufficiency of mere human statements has become fixed in the mind of the world.

That Hume's reasoning was illegitimate is certain; but this was because he refused to admit into his thought elements that were indispensable to the soundness of his premises and the correctness of his logical procedure. Looking only to the limitations and the fallibility of men, and reckoning upon the admitted uniformity of nature, he could reach no other conclusion.

Nor is it in the schools of skepticism and physical science alone that uncertainty prevails. The same condition confronts us wherever mere human agency, however honest and eager for the truth, interposes and gives formal statement and definition, to explain, to demonstrate the facts of our gospel. So soon as these are put into dogmatic shape, diversities of judgment, varieties of theological opinion and positive antagonisms of creed arise. The schools, the pupil, and the press offer to-day ample proof and illustration, while the contentions and controversies which have marked the history of the Church have become proverbial. If the knowledge of the only living and true God, and of Jesus Christ whom he sent, be made dependent upon such testimonies, and our eternal life hang upon this knowledge, we are sadly straitened. To what witness shall we go? What school shall we follow? What formula shall we use? We are

almost constrained to say with Amiel, "About Jesus we must believe no one but himself.   Certainly
we must accept the conclusion of the late Bishop
of Durham: "If it is not by the senses, so neither
is it by theological and scientific faculties that we
can apprehend God, can see the Father.   These
faculties may verify, may explain, may systematize;
but they cannot give the insight, cannot create the
belief.   I doubt whether the most elaborate proofs
of the being and attributes of God, the most subtle expositions of the evidences of Christianity have
done very much toward establishing even an intellectual assent.   I am quite sure that they have been
all but powerless in commanding a living, working
belief."

The gospels, the truest and most profound disclosures of human as well as divine nature, offer
us the best illustrations and strongest proofs of the
insufficiency of mere human testimony.   The incarnate life as there portrayed is confessedly
unique.   In all excellencies of character and wonders of achievement it is without peer.   It has given
the world its one supreme ideal of greatness and
beauty, standing out in unapproachable splendor
upon the background of patriarchal, legal, and
prophetic life—yea, of all antecedent historic life—
and flinging its glory upon the ages of apostolic

heroism and lighting up the shadows of the later centuries. As we look back upon that marvelous figure the halo is about his head and the ideal has emerged from the obscurity of the hard and narrow conditions in the midst of which he did his work. We can never even think of him as he appeared to the men of his time. Art has exhausted its resources in the effort to reproduce his form and features, and has only succeeded in offering to the wonder and worship of the world an idealized conception of what he ought to have been. We know him after the flesh no more. The Man of Sorrows, having no form nor comeliness, and no beauty that we should desire him, is forever gone from the thought and heart of men. Yet we know that he did not appear to his own generation as to us, and wonder at the blindness and stupidity which held the men of that day back from him. In Nazareth, the son of the carpenter, whose " mother and sisters are here with us," was an offense. He upbraids the cities in which his mighty works were done, Chorazin, Bethsaida, and even Capernaum, which was exalted unto heaven, because they repented not. When he came nigh to Jerusalem, he wept over the sacred city and with infinite pathos denounced against it the dreadful doom of utter destruction, because it

knew not the time of its visitation.   The multitudes
came to him not because they saw the sign, but
because they did eat of the loaves and were filled.
His own disciples, almost at the last hour of his
sojourn with them, he reproved as " fools and slow
of heart to believe."   It seems strange to us, and
from the point of view of these last days, we se-
cretly incline to say with Peter, " Be this far from
thee, Lord;" these things ought not so to have
been.   The contrast between the ideal and the
real, the thought of our time and the view of his
own period, is sharply drawn when we read the
inimitable, exquisite sketch of the " Character of
Christ," by an eminent preacher of the last generation outside the pale of intellectual orthodoxy.
It is the work of a master, and in lines of almost
perfect beauty sets before us the form of the Son
of Man as he appears from the open heavens, transfigured in the sight of the world.   Death and time
and history and unrecognized influences have done
their work, so that even Channing was constrained
to join the centurion in the confession, " Truly this
was, not only was, but is, the Son of God."

But then the human side dominated, and men
looked at him with only human eyes, incapable of
discerning the glory that Isaiah had seen.   Prophecy found its fulfillment in them.   Having eyes

they see not, and ears they hear not: neither do they understand with their heart. The organs which are cognizant of spiritual things were not awake in them. The natural man could not know the things of God; and the mystery of God, even the Father, and of Christ was hidden from them. Moral obliquity and intellectual incapacity were alike concerned in the failure.

All this might not have seemed so strange and even unnatural had it happened among the nations given to idolatry and imbruted by the abominations of idolatrous life. But he came unto his own. They were his own by covenant and by legal and prophetic training. Nothing had been wanting to educate and prepare them for his coming. Yet his own received him not. In spite of all that had gone before, they considered only which was seen of him in the flesh, put the fleshly interpretation upon it, could not behind the signs that he gave them see the things signified, and in the grossness of their mind demanded a sign from heaven quite other than that he was daily furnishing.

If ever the human understanding could by rational process be brought to the apprehension of the divine character of the Son of Man, it would surely have been in the case of the twelve disciples. In a peculiar sense they were his own, more intimately

so than the body of the Jewish people claimed for
him by the evangelist. He had chosen them and
called them to himself. Some of them had been
the disciples of John, the forerunner, and by him
had been prepared for the advent of the Messiah;
and perhaps all of them had heard, as had the
Jews from Jerusalem, John's testimony concerning
him. They had the faith of their forefathers,
quickened and purified by their baptism with water — John's baptism — unto repentance. They
were sober-minded men, eager and self-renouncing
in their pursuit of the truth. If any of them, as
Levi, had been under the sway of the passions and
vices of the world, the complete and final abandonment of them at His call sufficiently indicated
their emancipation from the blinding influence,
while former experience in the active, practical
concerns of life, sharpened their faculties and for-
bade hasty judgments under the impulse of enthu-
siasm or popular excitement. The Gospel of Mat-
thew is in evidence. Never were materials of such
sort handled in such sober and unimpassioned way.
These men were taught by the Lord himself in
public and in private. The mysteries of his kingdom which were spoken to the people in parables
were to them expounded plainly and in full. They
were brought into most intimate association with his

private and inner life; and in the extravagance of his love—to borrow Archdeacon Farrar's phrase—he lavished upon them the resources of his wonderful person. The bare synopsis of his work and words given us in the Gospels reveals a fullness of utterance and achievement that would seem to leave nothing to be desired. But to this must be added the " many other things that are not written in this book," the daily life of labor and prayer, the minute and careful instruction, and the awakening, purifying, and elevating power of all these, upon their moral and spiritual faculties. Nothing that could be conveyed through the regular channels to the mind of man was withheld. At the critical moment in his career and of their connection with him he brings them to the test. In the coasts of Cæsarea Philippi, remote from the disturbing influences of the multitudes, and free for the moment from the stimulating effect of his wonderful working, he asks them the question: " Whom do men say that I, the Son of man, am?" The tide of public opinion, moved by all the forces of his charter and work, had up to that time set in his favor. He was assigned a position of sanctity and of authority as teacher and prophet. Beyond this the mind of the people could not go. The varying temper and conscience affected the reason and

judgment of them all, and left him with an undefined rank among the men commissioned of God
for special service. Nothing more can ever be
looked for from the unaided mind of man. Its
highest culture, its keenest insight will never lift it
beyond its environments or force it from the proclivities, propensions, and affections inwrought into
the moral constitution. The differences among
men when they confront questions of this sort are
precisely those suggested in this interview.

"Whom say *ye* that I am?" A fuller light, a
deeper insight had been vouchsafed to them, and a
larger response was to have been expected. It was
given; and the first of the great confessions by
which the Church has honored the Son fell from
the lips of Peter: "Thou art the Christ, the son
of the living God." It was not the last, nor was
it the fullest except by implication and as interpreted by more profound and light-giving teachings
of later date. But such as it was, the Son of Man
immediately disclaims for it any human authority,
denies the power of "flesh and blood" to discover
or reveal him, and withdraws his Church at once
and forever from the sphere of human wisdom and
power and commits it exclusively to the one foundation laid in the supernatural revelation and apprehension of the truth of his person.

How limited was their conception of the meaning of the words they used appears directly when
Peter, upon the Lord's announcement of his coming humiliation and death, rebukes him and would
turn him from his purpose. The stern reply of
the Son of God shows that the apostle was still so
far out of sympathy with the mind of God that his
attitude was that of an adversary, and he was incapable of appreciating the work of God in and
through his Son. Nor does there seem to be
much advance from this point to the day of his
resurrection. The sharp contrasts of joy and sorrow, light and darkness, life and death, which he
continually set before them, puzzled and bewil-
dered them. They thought that he spake in parables. When, by gradual approaches, he led
them, all unknowing the way they took, to the supreme and final declarations of his work and of
his personal relations to the Father, they still
asked: "Show us the Father." And when the
darkness of the shameful death had covered them,
and intimation was brought of a possible recovery
from even that disaster, the strongest word that
they could speak was: "We hoped that it was he
which should redeem Israel." So incomplete, so
obscure was the testimony that until this hour these
chosen and trained witnesses were able to give.

The validity of human testimony lies at the foundation of all our knowledge and enters into the substance of our life. Our earliest lessons we take from those who have gone over the way before us. Instinctively we put faith in their words. We may find in later years that they were mistaken, or have willfully deceived us; but we do not therefore withdraw our confidence from the world with which we associate. To discredit all that is told us is to make life impossible. The verification in authorized and sure ways is, to most of us, impracticable; and, with whatever measures of reserve, we are content for the practical purposes of life to accept the results reached by those who have ability and opportunity for research.

The same is true in measure when we come to deal with the historical side of our gospel. The actual presence of Jesus of Nazareth in the world is as much matter of historical inquiry as that of Cæsar or Seneca. What he did and what he said may be reported with as much accuracy by eye and ear witnesses as the sayings of Socrates or the achievements of Alexander. These have their human side and their earthly setting, and the resources of criticism have been expended upon them without protest or objection from any of those to whom the Christ is most dear and most sacred. If this were all the contents of our gospel, we could be willing to let it stand upon the same ground as any other event or series of events in history, and ask for it the same sort and measure of faith that are accorded to the records of other times and places.

But, in truth, there are elements in this history as we all feel and many of us know, that put it in an exceptional position and charge it with a value immeasurably transcending that attaching to any other records. This inquiry does not look simply to the increase of the sum of human knowledge; nor does it propose to enlighten us from the experience of the past as to the errors to be avoided and the plans to be pursued in advancing the interests and regulating the affairs of this world. If the record of the gospel is to be believed, it has a higher significance and a purpose that reaches farther. It will not suffer us to restrict our thought (our knowledge) in either direction to the times and conditions of this present world. Turning back, it links us to the purpose and life "before the foundation of the world," which gave beginning, order, and meaning to all that was created or ever shall be. Turning forward, it projects us beyond the boundaries of time, through the episode of death, into the interminable ages of conscious, ordered, and organized life which it affirms to be the preordained consummation of all history and all life. The undated antecedent life is expressed to us in the incarnation; the ages to come hail us in the resurrection of the Son of God. All the power and possibilities of eternity are conveyed to us in the intenseness of the life that makes its advent in the stable of Bethlehem and passes away from mortal vision over the summit of the mount in the cloud that " received him out of their sight." All the hopes of all men center in his person. By right of his indefeasible relations to the world as " firstborn of the whole creation, . . . in whom all things consist," he gathers into himself the life of all the generations, bears it with him into the abysses of death, and having thus by himself purged our sins rises again, disburdened, emancipated, glorified, and ascends up where he was before, a High Priest, *the* High Priest of the universe, according to the power of an indissoluble life. " The Lamb of God that taketh away the sins of the world," he is forevermore the only life and light of men.

We can apply no canons of criticism to such statement of facts. It lies wholly beyond their range. We can trust no calculation of probabilities here. We can rely upon no inferences, no

deductions. No element of uncertainty must enter to confuse our faith. We can suspend the
issues of eternity involved in the reality and rectitude of our relations to Him upon no other than
"infallible proofs." The conscience - stricken
world cries out for assured forgiveness. The
groping, stumbling world, feeling its way in the
dark, longs for light. The dying world in its
agony of wretchedness pleads with unutterable
groanings for life. Never has the promise been
given it of forgiveness, life, light, except in Jesus
Christ. It will not be content with aught less than
the sure knowledge of him. It were a mockery
to offer less.

Among them that were born of women there
had not risen a greater than John the Baptist, and
he bare witness to the truth. But the question of
man's accountability for the truth could not be referred to the testimony of even John. He does
not trust to his own insight or discernment or the
sufficiency of his own faculties. "I knew Him
not," he said. His witness is to that which had
been communicated to him. It is hearsay. He
refers his disciples to Jesus himself to find out
who he is. He sent two of them, saying: "Art
thou he?" He did all that any mere human witness can ever do: he brought men to Christ. As-

signing to him the foremost place in the ranks of the prophets—nay, elevating him above the prophetic level, "more than a prophet"—Jesus yet declined to trust his character and claims to his testimony. If the highest form of human knowledge, clarified by unimpeachable integrity of character and broadened by intimate and familiar converse with the truest, most profound, and most far-reaching scriptures ever furnished for human counsel and instruction; if prophetic gifts beyond any ever bestowed upon sons of men; if an immediate commission charged with this special function—if all these combined could not give absolute and final validity to testimony, to whom shall we go?

Yet once more. It has already been said that the Son of God sent forth men as witnesses to himself after his ascension. The course of these lectures will later bring us to the consideration of the extent, meaning, and value of their testimony. It is enough to say now in anticipation that they did not commit the vindication of their gospel to the validity and sufficiency of their own statements. They were profoundly conscious of their own living, personal relations to their Lord; they were absolutely assured of the truthfulness of their presentation of his character and life—antecedent, incarnate, and ascended. They were bold and pronounced in their avowal that they had received from the Lord himself their commission to preach him and authority to establish and regulate the affairs of his Church. Yet they refused to have or exercise dominion over the faith of men and knew nothing among them but Jesus Christ and him crucified, that their " faith should not stand in the wisdom of men, but in the power of God." Their preaching was nothing unless it was " by [or in] the Holy Ghost sent forth from heaven." The " earthen vessels " were not taken account of. The word itself, as the very word of God, in demonstration of the Spirit and of power, was relied upon to work effectually in them that believe. It is the special characteristic of the apostolic ministry that it was separated as widely as possible from the arts and resources of this world's wisdom, and that just in proportion to the completeness of this separation was the absoluteness of their conviction. When the demands of controversy with the Jews and heathen brought into play the subtleties of the intellectual faculties, heresies arose which, for the most part, formed themselves upon the incomplete or enfeebled apprehension of the person of the Son of God by the mere human understanding. The spiritual vision was dimmed, and the true wit-

nesses—men who could not but speak the things
which they had seen and heard—were relegated
to comparative obscurity, while the Church visible
and regnant set itself to defining the indefinable
and explaining the inexplicable, asserted authority
over the thoughts of men, became the tyrant of
conscience, and ended by establishing a despotism
in the realm of mind and faith unparalleled in history and as far removed from the free and beneficent reign of the Son of God as the beast with
seven heads and ten horns in John's vision is from
the Lamb standing on Mount Sion.

The times have changed. Protestantism has
been at work and brought in freedom of thought
and liberty of conscience. We worship where we
will, as we will, and whom we will. Laxity of
faith has taken the place of intolerance; and the
world says that it matters not what a man believes,
only so that he be honest in his belief. Indiffer-
entism is very largely the characteristic of the
times. To this, with all the evil and danger attendant, it may safely be said that two things have
contributed: first, the loss of the consciousness
of sin; second, the loss of the vision of the Saviour. Sin has become only a synonym for vice
or crime, and a pure morality has been substi-
tuted for eternal life; so that the tremendous

forces expressed in the person and work of the
Son of God are deemed wholly unnecessary, and
the Saviour of the world is assigned an honor-
ary place at the head and center of a social, intellectual, and æsthetic realm known as the Church,
which he may adorn with his presence, but must
not perturb, distress, and humiliate by the shame
and horror of his cross. We have come perilous-
ly near to reducing the Church of the Son of God,
which he purchased with his own blood, to the
level of a purely natural and human association
for earthly purposes, dissolving its connections
with eternity and eliminating the supernatural element from character and life. But there are
still witnesses for him, men whose conversation
is in heaven, whose life is hid with him in God,
who have known sin and know the Saviour, and
who in the knowledge of the only true God and
of Jesus Christ whom he has sent have eternal
life. Believing on the Son of God, they have
the witness in themselves—a higher than any
human witness—and when they testify the things
which they have seen and heard, a truer and
diviner than themselves confirms and effectuates
their word.

Thus in brief the attempt has been made to show
that where the person and work of the Son of God

are in question no mere human testimony is sufficient.   He himself declines the best witness this
world could offer, even while he declares that he
bare witness to the truth.   *I* must have, and have,
greater witness than that of John.   He was a light
that consumed as it shone; and while the Jews for
a season exulted in that light, it soon flickered and
died away, and left the eternal verities of the person of the Son of God unlighted by any ray of
human wisdom or excellency.   Outside of that
narrow circle of paling and fading glory there was
no possible witness to the stupendous facts expressed in the incarnation.   The oracles of heathenism are dumb.   The votaries of the false faiths,
like the priests of Baal, cry out in the bitterness of
their passion, and torture themselves in their mad
eagerness to evoke some response to their questionings.   Nature   and   God   are   alike   silent.
There is neither voice, nor any to answer, nor any
that regardeth.   Nature has no answer to give,
and God is not to be worshiped by men's hands,
nor invoked by the wild outcries of disappointed
and wrathful sufferers.   Philosophy has settled
no question touching man's relation to the unseen,
and offers no solution-of the vexing problem of the
reconciliation between the infinite and the finite,
between God and the world.   Science in its pro-

foundest search and its widest reach has not
touched the outskirts of that realm to which the
Son of God belongs. The star of Bethlehem has
gone out of its sky, and the countless host of the
firmament still obscure the portals of light and
make no pathway for our coming Judge.

If we would satisfy our conscience and still the
clamors of our heart, we must withdraw into the
solitudes of the soul, look upon the transfigured
Son of man, lift our inner eye to the bright cloud
that settles down on him and all who are with
him, and turn our inner ear to the voice that comes
out of the cloud: "This is my beloved Son.
Hear ye him."

LECTURE II.

THE CONJOINT TESTIMONY OF THE FATHER AND THE SON.

(41)

II.

"I am one that bear witness of myself, and the Father that
sent me beareth witness of me." John viii. 18.

ANOTHER order of witnesses, higher than
any that this world could furnish, and apparently quite in keeping with the old order of divine movement, might have been called from that
broad region of. life that lies between the narrow-
ness of our condition and the fullness of the Godhead. Angels, by whom, as Stephen, Paul, and
the Epistle to the Hebrews affirm, the word of the
law was spoken, could have given strong confirmation to the claims of him who is Lord over all.
The intimacy of the relations of the Son of God
with the eternal world, as well as his earnest desire and purpose to save men, would seem to suggest the enlistment of such agencies in his service.
But our ways are not God's ways. Had he intended to effect his purpose by the display of
wonders and extraordinary powers, nothing more
would have been needed than the free employ-
ment of these ministers of his that " excel in

(43)

strength." The sweep of the legions that were
at the command of Christ would have given
speedy settlement to all questions affecting his
rights and powers. Indeed, he did not hesitate to
declare his purpose to use them to the utmost limit in the final judgment and disposition of affairs,
" when the Son of man shall come in his glory,
and all the holy angels with him." They shall
be the reapers, and theirs it shall be to sever the
wicked from among the just, and deliver them
over to the endurance of the penalty pronounced.
But in the process of his incarnate life there was a
marked avoidance of display and of all preternatural agencies that would lift himself above the
normal conditions of human life and unduly affect the mind, the conscience, and the spiritual
faculties of men. He had thrown the veil of the
" likeness of sinful flesh " over the majesty of his
person, and did not intend that it should be thrust
aside by demon or angel while he tabernacled on
earth. Only when it should be rudely rent in
twain by human hands, and the way into the holiest consecrated for us through his flesh, should
men come into that presence.

The seeming exceptions are rare. Angelic
ministrations, under this economy, appear only
when no other agency is available. Gabriel was

sent to Zechariah to announce the birth of the
forerunner and to Mary to declare that she
should be the mother of the Christ. Angels sang
to the shepherds the song of the advent, and sent
them to Bethlehem to find in the manger the babe
that should be "ruler in Israel." An angel of
the Lord appeared to Joseph in a dream to warn
him of the danger to the infant Jesus, and again
at the end of the sojourn in Egypt to bid him return to the land of Israel. After the long struggle
with the devil in the wilderness, angels came and
ministered to Christ. After the agony in the garden an angel appeared to strengthen him. An
angel rolled away the stone from the tomb on the
morning of the resurrection, and announced the
fact to the women who came to find his body.
As messengers from the courts of heaven they
came to bring the tidings of his birth and of his
resurrection to the chosen few, and as minister-
ing spirits they were at hand to sustain and comfort when the flesh could no longer bear the
weight of trial. But he never invoked them as
witnesses, nor appealed to their appearance in his
own behalf. On the one hand, the overpowering
rush of angelic forces would have been hopelessly
at variance with the moral and spiritual movement
involved in and essential to human salvation; and,

on the other, as concerning his own person, it was clearly his purpose to leave the settlement of the great question to the decision of the final and supreme tribunal, and appeal to his Father only in support of his claim. The dignity of his character, and the immensity of the work that he was to do, demanded the sanction and indorsement of the highest authority, and with nothing less than this would he attempt to satisfy the souls of men.

This seems to be a necessity when we consider that he refers his coming into the world, his work, his relations to men, his very affections and all the issues of his life in time and eternity, to the will of the Father and by utmost fullness and emphasis of statement makes him responsible for the whole. "The Father sent me." "I proceeded forth and came from God; neither came I of myself, but he sent me." "I came down from heaven, not to do mine own will, but the will of him that sent me." "My meat is to do the will of him that sent me, and to finish his work." "The words that I speak unto you I speak not of myself: but the Father that dwelleth in me; he doeth the works." "The Son can do nothing of himself, but what he seeth the Father do: for what things soever he doeth, these also doeth the Son likewise." From which he goes on to affirm the power to quicken the dead, and the authority to judge all men, as the Father's gift to him. His disciples were those whom the Father gave him, and "no man can come to me, except the Father which hath sent me, draw him." It is the Father's will that these should have everlasting life and that the Son should raise them up at the last day. His care and affection for those who came to him were because the Father gave them to him. "Thine they were, and thou gavest them me." "Those that thou gavest me I have kept."

Exceptional prophetic utterance or achievement might make appeal to the minds of men by its wonder, or its high ethical quality. But here the entire life, in its beginnings, in its impulses and affections, in its purposes and issues, in all its relations to God and men, to time and eternity, is referred immediately and continuously to the will, the working, and the indwelling of the Father. It is not merely a manifestation of wonders and signs, nor of a supreme ethical quality and purpose. In the entire process of his inner and outer life and in its consummation, it is the embodied expression of the Father. The attestation of the Father himself was needed to command the faith of the world. The place he thus assumed and the work he undertook required the entire authority of the Godhead.

On the one side, therefore, we must look for the most complete attestation that the Father could give to the Son; and on the other, we must expect to find it not in outbursts of energy which may measure the almightiness of God, nor in the blazing forth of splendors that may assert for the Son a glory passing that of all created things, but in the due and ordered ways of divine working, and under the restrictions and conditions of the incarnate life to which he subjected himself. For without such reserve the process of divine manifestation could not be brought into normal relation to the ethical character of men, and salvation would have been impossible.

Do we not too often in our eagerness to rescue men make the mistake of longing for, and even appealing to, some abnormal, extraordinary movement in nature or life, some wonderful outcome of the order, the providential order of human affairs, as a truer and more satisfactory demonstration of the presence and power of God among men, than daily life and the common course of events can furnish? We forget that the long series of seemingly insignificant circumstances, influences, movements which bring about the great

result are as truly under divine direction as the
issue can be; and indeed that the failure to discern him in the antecedents is almost certainly
fatal to any ethical, saving result in the consequent. Do we not forget, too, how constantly
and earnestly our Lord taught men to look for
God in the ordinary course of nature and the triv-
ial occurrences of common life? The grass of the
field, the lily, the rock, the sand, the sparrow, the
morning and the evening light, and all the vast va-
riety of natural phenomena were so many syllables
written by the finger of God, for the children of
men to spell out. He refused the sign from heav-
en, because, if they could not read the signs given
in earth, how hopeless to expect them to interpret
the mysterious symbols from the skies! "If I
have told you earthly things, and ye believe not,
how shall ye believe, if I tell you of heavenly
things?" We may put a due estimate upon such
marvels as appear at Sodom and Sinai, and stand
in awe in the presence of the possibilities of wrath
and judgment declared in them; but we shall, like
Israel, put ourselves at greater distance from God,
and beg to hear his voice no more. Such displays
belong to an inferior economy, and make their appeal to the early generations and imperfectly developed faculties. When the fullness of time was

4

come and the period of childhood training was passed, God spoke in other forms and with fuller utterance. We therefore look for the sort of testimony most in agreement with the regular and uniform movement of God upon and among men and that most surely expresses his mind and purpose. The stars were not swung out of their courses to make a pathway for the coming of the Son of God. The angels of God worshiped him, but a woman's bosom was his first tabernacle here, and the swaddling clothes, the manger, and the surroundings of a simple country village tell of the reality and the lowliness of his human beginnings. As was his entrance, so was his career; and within these limitations he intended men to see the Father and to hear the voice of God.

We may now read the meaning of the text: "I" that stand among you in human form "am he that beareth witness of myself;" but not alone. "The Father that sent me beareth witness of me." The witness was joint and inseparable. The Son could not give witness of himself without the Father; nor could the Father bear witness without the Son. How interdependent they are, each upon the other, for the manifestation of himself, is evident in every instruction that Jesus gives concerning the Godhead. In connection with the assertion of his judicial power over the cities that repented not when he came to them, he utters his thanksgiving to the Father that the things about himself were not committed to the wisdom and prudence of men, but revealed to babes, and withdraws them from the sphere of human research by the declaration: "No man knoweth the Son, but the Father; neither knoweth any man the Father, save the Son, and he to whomsoever the Son will reveal him." Agreeing therewith, it is said in the beginning of the gospel of John: "No man hath seen God at any time; the only begotten Son, which is in the bosom of the Father, he hath declared him." For the understanding of himself, it is necessary that men should hear from the Father and learn—in the words of prophecy, "be taught of God "—so that, in his own words, "No man can come to me, except the Father which hath sent me draw him." In its most positive form he sums up and reiterates the truth among his later teachings: "I am the way, the truth, and the life. No man cometh unto the Father but by me. He that hath seen me hath seen the Father. I am in the Father and the Father in me." Through all his course, while expending the wealth of divine wisdom and lavishing the resources of divine power upon men, he charged them with sin because of their rejection of him, and referred it to their failure to discern and understand God: "Ye know neither me, nor my Father: if ye had known me, ye should have known my Father also."

It thus behooves us to consider that the Christ of our gospel is not a disclosure made on the human side of his life of certain characters of God, hitherto unknown, which bring him into nearer relationship to men than the world had believed possible; rather he is the final and complete revelation of the Godhead. In him meet all the divine personalities, Father, Son, and Holy Spirit, each witnessing to the other, and so bringing the full weight of divine authority for the confirmation of the truth by which men are saved.

In my native city there is a Church of the denomination which refuses Jesus Christ his rightful place in the Godhead, with the inscription over its entrance: τω μόνω θεῷ, "To the only God." The inscription is misplaced. It belongs to the altars where all "men honor the Son even as they honor the Father." "Probably no philosophy was ever able to rest ultimately in the Deistic or Unitarian conception of God; that is to say, every attempt merely to regard the divine Being in simplicity as one has ended in Pantheism, or else has been obliged to develop into some multiformity, so as to bring God and the world into relation." What is true, as thus stated by a Bampton lecturer, of philosophy, applies with equal force to the ethical and practical side of human life. The conscience and the heart, when appealed to and charged with obligation and the fervor of devotion, will not be satisfied to answer the demand unless there be some attendant assurance that the relations upon which these depend belong to the life of the God who asserts his authority over us. They will only be felt as binding when we can trace them back to their antitypes and beginnings in the divine nature, and recognize them as reflections within our sphere and measure of elements and forces existent in the Godhead. Our gospel does not offer us a God void of contents and colorless in the absolute simplicity of his being, in application to whom the terms Father and Son—or any other terms of relation—are meaningless, or have only figurative meaning, much too remote and indistinct to bring him within the life of men, though they be called sons. "The only God" of the gospel is continent of Fatherhood and Sonship in the unity of the Spirit. The exclusion of either is the denial of the only living and true God; for "whosoever denieth the Son, the same hath not the Father: he that confesseth the Son hath the

Father also." Wherever the interior relations of
the Godhead are contemplated in the New Testament—the Old Testament is out of the question,
because it does not claim to be a complete and
final revelation of God or of aught else—and especially in the writings of John, the distinction between the absolute and indefinable term " God "
and the relative, mutually dependent, and inseparable terms " Father" and " Son" is almost invariably observed. "No man hath seen God at any
time; the only begotten Son, which is in the bosom of the Father, he hath declared him.'" It is
almost the exact parallel of Paul's teaching of
Christ to the Colossians, " Who is the image of the
invisible God, the firstborn of every creature;"
and of the writing to the Hebrews, "God . . . .
hath spoken unto us by his Son . . . the
brightness of his glory, and the express image of
his person." The truer rendering is, of course,
that of the Revised Version, "the effulgence
[shining forth] of his glory and the very image
of his substance."

Our Lord uses the term " Father " save when
indicating his own relation to the Godhead as such,
or when speaking to men the truths that affect their
relations to God simply. " Not that any man
hath seen the Father save he which is of God, he

hath seen the Father." In the supreme crisis of his life, when the consciousness of human suffering overlaid the consciousness of divine relations, he used the Old Testament speech: " My God, my God, why hast thou forsaken me?" In the next moment his final triumph is signalized by the word, " Father, into thy hands I commend my spirit." So also we have the same result when we compare " I proceeded forth and came from God " with the expression " The only begotten Son, which is in the bosom of the Father." In all the New Testament God is " invisible," whom " no man hath seen, nor can see," " dwelling in the light which no man can approach unto." As the Father, in the inner distinctions and functions of the divine life, he is the fountain of Godhead from whom it eternally flows into the person of the Son, the express image of his substance, in and through whom all the glory of God shines forth, and by whom alone the counsels of God are made known and his purposes executed.

It is not the occasion for a discussion, or even more than a cursory statement of the scriptural doctrine of the triune God. Nor is it intended to state it in the form of a " speculative opinion, a metaphysical definition in scholastic dogma," but as a living truth, " a fact which transcends all experience, which is of no special time or place, which is eternal in the heavens. The substance of it is that there is one God, eternal, omnipotent, all-wise, all-good; and that this one God, taking into the account the inadequacies of human language and the poverty of human thought, is most correctly conceived of and spoken of as Father, Son, Spirit, as Three in One."

So much is necessary that we may have understanding of what our gospel teaches of God and of the nature and force of the testimony to which it makes appeal in behalf of the Son.

1. The conjoint testimony of the Father and Son is in confirmation of the ancient monotheistic teaching of one God, Creator of all things. He is the absolutely inexhaustible Fountain and Source of being, motion, life. "In him we live, and move, and have our being."

2. God is eternal. He is not under any limitation or reckonings of time or measurements of space. In the expressive phrase of Isaiah, he is the "high and lofty One that inhabiteth eternity."

3. God is the Upholder and Director of all things. He preserves all things, assigns them their place and time, and orders and guards their movement. Not a sparrow falls to the ground without him.

4. God is all-wise. In the ends that he proposes

he is determined by the perfections of his own nature, and in his methods adjusts the resources of his illimitable domain to his purpose with absolute accuracy.

5. God is all-good. He finds his own infinite delight in the exercise of his own energies as expressive of kindly, orderly, and beneficent dispositions, and in a measure repeats and reproduces himself in all the works of his hands.

6. He is all-righteous. Rectitude is original with him, and the order of the universe and the ethical consciousness and relations of intelligent beings are expressions in their proportion of his own sense and love of rightness.

7. These are all elements in his self-consciousness, and find expression in his will and works, so declaring the invisible, illimitable, eternal God to be personal. The word may be inadequate, even defective. What human speech is adequate? What terms are not defective when we undertake to translate into forms of human thought the realities of the eternal life? The things which Paul heard in the third heaven were unspeakable, not possible for a man to utter. How shall we hope, then, to give utterance to the characters of the life above all heavens, filling all things so that heaven and the heaven of heavens cannot contain him?

Only, however inadequate, however defective the word may be, it is, in its use, the only word that expresses the highest essential character of intelligent, self-conscious being—the highest order of being known, and, considering what we are, possible to be known to us. The *living* God is by necessity of thought—shall I not rather say by necessity of consciousness?—to us the personal God.

8. In entire agreement thus far with the old Hebrew monotheism, the testimony of the gospel transcends that sphere and declares the one living and true God to be Father and Son. In a certain very real sense the term "Father" is applied to the relationship between God and men, and with greater intenseness of meaning and constant emphasis in the Christian economy it is used to indicate the more intimate relation to God into which men are brought by Jesus Christ. "Ye are all the children of God by faith in Christ Jesus." "Because ye are sons, God hath sent forth the Spirit of his Son into your hearts, crying, Abba, Father." In these cases the relation is mediated by Jesus Christ. Only in the person of the Son of God is it immediate and expressive of essential and eternal oneness of nature and being. By every token the poetic and sentimental as well as

the mediate and derivative sense of the term is excluded, and the deeper reality of the original, essential, and eternal communication of the nature and substance of the Godhead from the Father to the Son declared in the testimony of the Father and the Son. Our Lord uses the name when speaking to his disciples of their place and interest in the divine administration. "Your Father knoweth that ye have need of these things." "How much more shall your heavenly Father give the Holy Spirit to them that ask him!" But he never gives them the place that he himself holds, and always refers their right to his own relation to them. They would never have known the Father but for him. "The only begotten Son, which is in the bosom of the Father, he hath declared him." He was their Father only as he was first his own and as they were his." "I ascend unto my Father, and your Father"—just as he discloses their relation to the Godhead through himself—"to my God, and your God." His own Father and God first and supremely, and theirs because they were his.

9. In the economy of the Godhead, while the Father is the Fountain of all being and energy, he does nothing but by the Son. Whether known as the Word (*Logos*), the Image of the invisible

God, or the Son, by him were all things made, and without him was not anything made that hath been made. In him all things consist, and he upholdeth all things by the word of his power. So complete is the unity, so exhaustive the relation that "what things soever the Father doeth, these the Son also doeth in like manner," until in the final event, the spiritual quickening of men, the resurrection of the dead and the universal judgment shall complete the purpose of God, and the Son shall finish the work which the Father hath given him to do.

10. The testimony further and finally declares that the revelation is made, not to satisfy human desire for knowledge, to elevate and enlarge the intellectual capabilities of men, but that the world might be saved. "He shall save his people from their sins," was the preannounced meaning of his coming; that repentance and remission of sins should be preached in his name was his own final interpretation of his life to his disciples.

These statements may give us the clue to the nature of the testimony borne to the world in this behalf. To appreciate it we ought to take account of what is offered to our acceptance and faith outside the Christian sphere. It must not, however, be forgotten that the living God, though he suffered all nations to walk in their own ways, yet left not himself without witness among them, and that the Word "was the true Light, which lighteth every man that cometh into the world." There have, therefore, always been elect souls, seekers after God, among the Gentiles, who, having not the law, have done the things contained in the law, and " shall come from the east and the west and from the north and the south, and shall sit down in the kingdom of God." How many or how few, God only knows. They are enough to have a special place assigned them in the records of God's revelation and must be excluded from our estimate of the antichristian or unchristian world.

For the rest, the story of heathen thought and worship is given in brief but terrible statement in the beginning of the Epistle of Paul to the Romans. When they knew God they repressed the knowledge in their impiety and unrighteousness, and refused to glorify him as God. The natural and inevitable consequence came upon them in vain and false conceptions and darkened and imbruted understanding. Then followed the fearful degeneracy into idolatry, with all its attendant abominations and perversions and abuse of nature until God gave them over to a reprobate mind, a rejected, worthless reason, incapable of discerning the things that were befitting. By their fruits they are known. This witness is true. Heathenism to-day, except where it has been touched and modified by Christian influence, is as Paul described it. Not all the genius of poetry can transmute this dense darkness into light. The subtlest and most thorough philosophical research must fail to discover any true conception of God, or of aught that should be worshiped in all the systems of faith and service in heathendom. Gods many and lords many, naturalism, dualism, polytheism, fetichism, agnosticism, pantheism, and fate, with their kindred moral or immoral qualities and their appropriate social environment, you will find in all these lands; and it may be, here and there, at wide intervals, among the countless symbols of false worship, an altar obscurely placed with the unintelligible inscription, "To the Unknown God." It is the witness of a divine retribution upon the alienated heart of the nations.

Within the compass of Christian light it is no less true that "whosoever denieth the Son, the same hath not the Father." Divorce the two, refuse to the Son the place given him in the gospel in the economy of the divine life, and there is left a purely intellectual conception of God, a metaphysical abstraction which makes no appeal to the heart, does not satisfy the conscience, and commands no worship. When men import into the term all that the culture and inevitable Christian atmosphere of our later times compel them to include in it, and strip it of the anthropomorphisms which they so much dread and of the accidents of human thought, God passes into the region of the things that cannot be known or even thought. Agnosticism is the boast of abysmal ignorance to which men of our day have descended. If not absolutely " without God," certainly without God in the world.

Another form of the effort to satisfy the demand of the mind for God, is found in the deism which recognizes the existence of a First Cause whose interest in and connection with the affairs of created things ceased when they were fixed in their ordained paths and furnished with the laws according to which they should proceed.

Pantheism, in its purest form, as given by Spinoza, recognizes God as the only substance and the sum total of things as God. The distinction between the Creator and his works is abolished; or, properly speaking, there could be no works and no creation. As there is no God apart from nature, nature must be eternal, or the element of eternity must be eliminated from the conception of God. Personality may not be predicated.

Positivism refuses any place in the realm of human knowledge for metaphysical and theological conceptions, sneers at the absolute and unconditioned, the unknown and unknowable of agnosticism, and then turns upon itself and erects its temples and altars and offers its worship to a hazy apotheosized humanity, which may mean an ideal conception of the race, in the highest possibilities of its total being, or something of Carlisle's hero worship, a calendar of select positive saints, or the actual life of humanity in all its phases and in all its stages, with its sins and its sorrows, its weaknesses and its woes, its aspirations, its heroic achievements, its failures, its degradation, and its utter and hopeless humiliation in death. It refuses the worship due to the one faultless and perfect type and ideal of all human and divine excellence and glorifies the tarnished reputation of men who have long since rotted in the grave and left but an indistinct memory. The incense of that worship is the scent of the charnel house.

It is needless to recount the varieties of speculation and theory upon which men have fallen in due retribution for their abandonment of historic fact and divine revelation. They furnish material

for intellectual exercise for the few, and have no
practical significance except as they turn men
away from the truth and lead to hardness of heart
and reprobacy of mind. It is with the practical
side of the question that we are specially concerned. For what we see and know is that as
men refuse to "honor the Son as they honor the
Father" the deeper and truer ethical distinctions
are lost, the finer and purer moral qualities give
way to conventional and secular estimates, conscience adjusts itself to its environment and sin is
no more felt to be exceeding sinful. The only
link of connection between the divine and human,
the eternal and the temporal, is broken, and the
world, eccentric, swings away from its orbit, and
sweeps on into the unexplored and pathless regions
of outer darkness. In its bitterness of woe the
heart cries out, but there is no answer. The way
to the throne is lost. No rigor of Stoicism, no
careless epicurean vaunt, will suffice in the crises
of human experience. When the horrors of the
present time and the awe of the dreadful future
are upon us we want to look into the face and hear
the voice of One who can answer our desperate
demand, "Show us the Father" with the unerring truth and divine authority of the Son: "He
that hath seen me hath seen the Father."

5

Let us turn again to our testimony and see upon what this truth and authority rest. It assumes that there is a possibility of direct communication between God and man. It is against all the teaching that has elevated, inspired, and given hope to men that God may be known and reached only by argument and inference. The witness is that he is so near akin to us, that we are so truly made in his image that by normal and congenial methods real converse may be had between him and us. Like almost every other great truth, it was flashed out in syllables through the darkness of human history under the old dispensation; and a few men, the prophets of the future, read them and lived by them. Sometimes, as when the angels came to Abraham at Mamre, in living form he appeared and talked with men " as a man with his friend." Sometimes, as on cloud-girt and lightning-guarded Sinai, he came with all the apparel and attendance of nature in her most majestic aspect, and in tones as awful and far-reaching as " the voice of mighty thunderings" proclaimed his presence and his law. Now in the distinct but undefined speech to the Chaldean, Abram, and now in the still small voice to the prophet in the solitude of Horeb, he gives command to go on their missions of world-wide import. In whatever way of approach, or with whatever voice he spake, to those who heard him all things thenceforth had a new meaning. Life had a sanctity and a glory before unknown. Like the patriarch at Bethel they said: "The Lord is in this place." They read his words in nature, and the heavens and the earth were full of his glory. God was not afar off, but nigh at hand—nearer than their own thoughts. In the word of a still higher inspiration he was "over all and through all and in them all." To this answered a faculty in men capable of hearing his voice and a spirit to understand him. "There is a spirit in man: and the inspiration of the Almighty giveth them understanding." The sin of the world then as now was that seeing they saw not and hearing they heard not, neither did they understand with their heart. The seers and prophets interpreted him to the world, and the world received not their word. That these were exceptional instances does not militate against the assumption that the faculty itself is human—is not the exclusive property of any class or of any individuals, but belongs to man as man. There are exceptional developments of faculty in art. Michael Angelo and Raphael are not specimens of the average man. Only one in a century—in ten centuries, it may be—attained to their insight, to

their breadth, power, and accuracy of vision, to
their skill, their perfect use of their faculties.
But nobody looks beyond the normal quality and
possibility of human nature for the explanation of
their genius and the interpretation of their work.
It was precisely because they were more profoundly human, more thoroughly identified with the very
spirit and substance of our humanity than the rest
of us that they were able to do so much. Their
kinship with all men, with man as man, developed
in them faculties that lay latent in others and enabled them to appeal to rudimentary organs and
possibilities of inner sense of which men would,
but for such as they were, have been forever un-
conscious.

That there was something more than the merely
natural, material, visible—what the cant of later
days calls the positive—in such wonders of art as
the " Transfiguration," the " Last Judgment " on
the wall of the Sistine Chapel, and the more than
heroic figure of Moses at the tomb of Julius II. is
freely conceded. It is just in proportion as they
quicken within us the sense of the supernatural
that their real beauty and power are appreciated;
and it was because these masters were conscious
that at bottom, in his innermost consciousness, man
is linked to the eternal and when, even for a mo-

ment, relieved from the oppression of the material and sensuous instinctively reaches after the unseen and the infinite, that they dared to attempt through the forms of art the expression, or at least the suggestion of divine things. The response to their appeal we know. By the same tests we try all who claim the Master's degree in the world of arts, letters, or, it may be said reverently, religion. The human appeal is never complete until it is reenforced and supplemented by the divine. The divine call can never attract and save unless it come by natural channels and reach the normal faculties of our humanity.

It is in keeping with this that no stress is laid upon any specific form of divine manifestation under the economy of preparation. Angelic ministry under aspects little if at all variant from those of our humanity; voices indistinguishable from human utterance; natural phenomena; the cloud that covered the tabernacle and filled the temple; the visions to patriarch, seer, and prophet; dreams; and the insensible and indefinable movement upon the spirit that would admit no answer and would not be resisted—any and all ways by which man might be approached without violence done to his nature were indifferently used. It seems to have been the purpose of God to link himself in human

thought and sentiment with every form of nature
and every feature of our environment, to make us
feel

> A presence that disturbs us with the joy
> Of elevated thoughts ; a sense sublime
> Of something far more deeply interfused,
> Whose dwelling is the light of setting suns
> And the round ocean and the living air,
> And the blue sky, and in the mind of man:
> A motion and a spirit, that impels
> All thinking things, all objects of all thought,
> And rolls through all things. ·

If abnormal and extraordinary agencies were
employed, it was rather for wrath and judgment,
as in Sodom's ruin and the destruction of the As-
syrian army, when the saving work was no longer
in contemplation; and even then the awful stroke
was given apparently through such exceptional
agencies of nature as these " ministers of his that
excel in strength" could command. The light-
nings of God's heaven, the volcanic forces of
earth, the swiftly walking pestilence, and even the
sword of the nations, told—as they still tell to men
who will hear—that God is " over all and through
all."

In all these the essential was to reach the conscience and the heart. For, first of all, the ethical
conviction is a disclosure of God. The sense of

obligation and the sense of responsibility which
enter into the constitution of the conscience are
inseparable from the conviction of divine relations.
I can do no better here than quote the words of
the Bishop of Durham (Lightfoot) when, dwelling
upon the language of his great predecessor, Bishop Butler, in the last moments of his life: "It is
an awful thing to appear before the Moral Gov-
ernor of the world," he said. "The same
thought which thus accompanied him in his pas-
sage to eternity had dominated his life in time—
this consciousness of an Eternal Presence, this
sense of a Supreme Righteousness, this conviction
of a Divine Order, shaping, guiding, disposing all
the intricate vicissitudes of circumstance and all
the little lives of men—enshrouded now in a dark
atmosphere of mystery, revealing itself only in
glimpses through the rolling clouds of material
existence, dimly discerned by the dull and partial
vision of finite man, questioned, doubted, denied
by many, yet visible enough even now to the eye
of faith, working patiently but working surely,
vindicating itself ever and again in the long results
of time, but awaiting its complete and final vindication in the absolute issues of eternity; the truth
of all truths, the reality of all realities, the one
stubborn, steadfast fact, unchangeable while all

else is changing; this Presence, this Order, this Righteousness, in the language of Holy Scripture, this Word of the Lord, which shall outlive the solid earth under foot and the starry vault overhead." It was under the resistless pressure of that same dominating conviction that Bishop Butler wrote of " the Author and Cause of all things, who is more intimately present to us than anything else can be, and with whom we have a nearer and more constant intercourse than we can have with any creature."

Both the great bishops were right. For conscience, our ethical faculty, deals chiefly with the rectitude by which man is put in relation not only with his fellows, but primarily with God. The changing values of our nature can furnish no fixed standards of the worth of what we are or what we do; and obligation, withdrawn from its divine relations, is emptied of all notion of authority, determined by sentiment or sensitiveness and measured by utilitarian or hedonistic views, or instincts of the individual or society. Responsibility is referred to no absolute law and looks to no righteous account and estimate of ourselves under that law; but emerges only at the call of an armed public opinion, stirred into activity by the solicitations of self-interest. No *data* of ethics will suffice for the

demands of conscience that do not include as their
first postulate a righteous Ruler who orders the affairs of men with an absolute authority, and reveals
himself to us as the Supreme Judge, from whose
decisions there is no appeal. ·The first recorded
utterance of God to man was in the exercise of
authority and the announcement of law: "Thou
mayest" and "Thou shalt not." The next approach was in the enforcement of penalty and the
establishment of new conditions of life upon the
same basis of inexorable righteousness. Nor has
he ever since come to men, Job of old and Peter
of later time in the presence of that awful majesty
being witnesses, without producing such conviction
of absolute rectitude as reduced to hideous defor-
mity their highest ideal of individual and personal
righteousness. Nor on the other hand has there
ever been such a conviction of righteousness without that awful sense of the presence of the righteous God. The sense of righteousness, a true
conscience, is God's first revelation of himself to
every man.

In final realization of such intimations the first
disclosures of the Son of Man were in the realm of
conscience. He took in hand the work of the Baptist, and repeating his call to repentance, sent it
sounding into hitherto unexplored depths of human

consciousness. He translated law into life, the letter into the spirit, swept away the " shadow of things to come," and brought into full relief the " very image." He refused the standard of conventionalisms and filled out and perfected the inadequate and imperfect requirements of the Mosaic institute. He opened up in the way of beatitude possibilities of inward righteousness and perfect life absolutely independent of all environment until men began to feel that of a truth the kingdom of heaven was at hand. His person and his work exhibited such a complete embodiment and exercise of righteousness that hypocrisy was aghast and gnashed its teeth against him, and true and honest souls were abashed and awed, and joined in the cry and confession of Peter, " Depart from me, O Lord! for I am a sinful man!" Legal formulas, rabbinical pretensions, philosophical subtleties, and ethical theories vanish away in the presence of this incarnation of the righteousness of God. From that time, in spite of the cross and the grave—or rather shall we not say because of them? —and in spite of all the arrogance of this world's wisdom, the awakened conscience falls in his presence with the adoring cry: " My Lord and my God." Righteousness is felt to be the attribute and manifestation of the personal—the only living and true God, and is revealed perfectly only in Jesus Christ whom he has sent.

Again, the very relation of Father and Son, one and inseparable, declares the inherent quality, the essential attribute, of the divine nature to be love. "The Father loveth the Son, and showeth him all things that himself doeth." The partial and finite affection which finds expression in the best forms and highest relations of our human life are but blurred shadows of the real, true, and infinitely perfect love in the interior life of the Godhead. The oneness of being and attribute, the eternal communication to the Son of all the energy and excellence of the Father, pass our human knowledge. But in this is the ground and motive of all divine movement in the creation, and still more explicitly in our redemption. "God is love:" in himself, for the Father loveth the Son; and through the Son, in all his relations to the world, "for God so loved the world, that he gave his only begotten Son." It was impossible to repress the Father's relation to men and put that name upon their lips without quickening in them the sense of the love inherent in it. Through all the channels of the incarnate life there came to the world such streams of sympathy, such volumes of tender affection, such wealth of devotion and self-sacrifice

as had never been imagined in the loftiest flights
of philanthropy or called out by the urgencies of
the most intimate affection. His entire life, within and without, was a sacrifice, on one side, to
the will of the Father which sent him; and on the
other, to his love for those whom the Father gave
him. The incarnation of the Son is the absolutely
perfect expression of the Father's love. Therefore said John, "He that loveth not, knoweth not
God; for God is love;" and therefore we may
say that the truest and fullest revelation of God is
made when "the love of God is shed abroad in
the heart." The order given is a true one. Righteousness is first. God could not be love were he
not righteous. Conscience must first consent to
the law and principle of eternal rectitude before
it can recognize and appreciate the reality and
wealth of divine love.

The First Epistle of John, supposed by many
to have been written as a kind of preface or introduction to his Gospel, brings out the light of revelation as expressed in these two, righteousness
and love. They are never disjoined. Righteousness demands the propitiation; righteous love furnishes it. The righteous propitiation is the Advocate of the sinner with the loving Father. And
the heart of the forgiven sinner is quickened into

love and has the assurance that it has passed from death unto life. Thus again, by conjoint testimony, the Father and Son in their perfect oneness in love and by their manifestation and communication of righteous love through the incarnate Son reveal each the other. "He that dwelleth in love dwelleth in God."

The incarnation of the Son of God is the historical expression to the world of the intimate relations between God and the spirit of man, and the direct and immediate intercourse between them. "In the likeness of sinful flesh," he reaches the entire body of human faculties, and through these regularly constituted channels delivers truth, righteousness, and love in such fullness and with such energy as can fail of effect only when the channels are obstructed, the faculties deadened. It may be questioned if God could have spoken fully and finally to the understanding, the conscience, and the heart of men except through the divinely ordered ways of human relationship. The flesh may have been as the veil of the temple concealing the glory of the indwelling presence; but from behind the veil the voice of God was heard. Certainly the only way into the holiest is the new and living one through the vail, his flesh. The Word became flesh, and dwelt among us, and we beheld his glory. The personal life of our humanity is brought through the incarnate Son into due and direct relation and converse with God. To the opened sense the Father reveals the Son; to the pure in heart the Son brings the vision of God.

The Gospels record two instances of special and direct testimony given by the Father: one at his baptism, the other at the transfiguration. In these two special instances the whole line of direct testimony of the Father culminates, and, in agreement with its personal character, finds expression in articulate utterance. It is again and again the Word made manifest. "Jesus cometh from Galilee to the Jordan unto John, to be baptized of him." In his own words, "Thus it becometh us to fulfill all righteousness." Thus it became John to fulfill his ministry by the communication through its ordained rite of all its prerogative and power to his great successor. "There cometh one after me mightier than I." The prophetic function, which as to its old economic form and character had its consummation in John, was by him transmitted to Jesus. The word of the Baptist, "Repent," was also the first word of the Son of Man. Thus it became him to receive the investment by recognized ordinance with all the

function and power of the old dispensation intensified and spiritualized by the descent of the Spirit, which remained upon him. It was his inaugu-
ration into and endowment for his prophetic and
mediatorial ministry. Something more than the
highest priestly and prophetic authority was needed for such an investiture. As in reference to
John's witness he said, "I receive not testimony
from man;" so here he would say, "I receive
not authority from man." The Spirit was to
John the token, as he himself declared, referring
to the divine Word that had commissioned him:
"He that sent me to baptize with water, the same
said unto me, Upon whom thou shalt see the Spirit descending, and remaining on him, the same is
he which baptizeth with the Holy Ghost." But
for the final authentication of his mission this was
not sufficient for the Son of God. To meet his
demand, the heavens were divided, the veil that
covered the holy place of the Most High was torn
asunder, and from within in articulate utterance
came the word that summed up all the revelation
of law and prophecy, of nature and history:
"This is my beloved Son, in whom I am well
pleased. The complete conjunction of the divine
and human in the person of the Jesus who received baptism at John's hands was declared;

and the incarnation of the Son of God was affirmed as the ground of his authoritative ministry
to the world.

Once again when the disclosure of his divine
Sonship had been made and received as never before, and he was about to enter the shadows that
deepened upon him as he went down into the val-
ley of humiliation, he withdrew himself with chosen disciples into the mountain solitudes of Hermon
and was " transfigured before them." It was not
now the dove, as the visible symbol of the Spirit
remaining upon him and declaring his endowment
for his ministry, but the majesty of his own person, breaking in its splendor through the flesh and
even the homely garb of his human form, that
proclaimed the intimacy of his relation with the
eternal world. But for that sacrificial ministry to
which he had devoted himself, and which was the
theme of converse with prophet and lawgiver and
the reason and explanation of this manifestation
of his glory, he required once again the seal and
attestation of his Father. The " bright cloud "—
the shekinah of the old covenant, in whose presence the high priest offered the blood of atonement, and from which he received the word of
absolution for the people—overshadowed them,
and from it came the voice that had been heard

on the banks of the Jordan, "This is my beloved Son; hear him." Most appropriately Peter, whose perplexed mind above all others needed such settlement, turns back to this scene in his later years as the confirmation of his faith: "We have not followed cunningly devised fables, when we made known unto you the power and coming of our Lord Jesus Christ, but were eyewitnesses of his majesty. For he received from God the Father honor and glory, when there came such a voice to him from the excellent glory, This is my beloved Son, in whom I am well pleased. And this voice which came from heaven we heard, when we were with him in the holy mount."

The complement and completion of this authentication of his mission and work as High Priest is given in those last days when the horror of the cross had begun to vex and trouble his soul: "Now is my soul troubled; and what shall I say?" Here, too, as at the baptism and the transfiguration, his prayer broke the silence of the heavens and the response of the Father comes in terms that he interpreted for the sake of those that stood by him: "I have both glorified it, and will glorify it again."

All these are but signs like every divine work within the sphere of time and sense, and signify to

6

us the presence and working of God in the person of his Son in our flesh. They are only needful to complete the round of divine testimonies, and assure us that there is no way of approach to our nature by which God has not come, and to confirm our belief that Jesus, the man of Nazareth, is the Son of God, and that believing we may have life in his name.

In conclusion the sum of the things spoken is: (1) That the final appeal of Jesus Christ in the authentication of his person and mission is to the Father; (2) that the Father and Son witness each to the other and that their testimony is conjoint and not separate—so that no man cometh to the Són except the Father draw him, and no man cometh to the Father but by the Son; (3) that the testimony agrees with the monotheistic teaching of the Hebrew Scriptures in their affirmation of one personal, eternal Creator and Upholder of all things, all-wise, all-righteous, and all-good; (4) that this witness transcends and completes the antecedent revelation in declaring the personality of the Father, Son, and Spirit in the unity of the Godhead; (5) that it reveals the Son as the exhaustive expression of the Father's will, and executor of his purpose; (6) that this entire manifestation and incarnation of God contemplates the salvation of men; (7) and finally, that this testimony presupposes the possibility of God's approach to man, and faculties in man capable of receiving and responding to divine communications. In the integrity and normal and healthful exercise of these faculties is the knowledge of God, man's eternal life assured; and to quicken and restore them to full activity is the purpose of the incarnation. "I am come that they might have life, and that they might have it more abundantly."

LECTURE III.

THE TESTIMONY OF THE WORKS.

III.

THE TESTIMONY OF THE WORKS.

"The words that I speak unto you I speak not of myself: but the Father that dwelleth in me, he doeth the works. Believe me that I am in the Father, and the Father in me: or else believe me for the very works' sake." John xiv. 10, 11.

THE conjoint testimony of Father and Son given out of the heavens and on the side of the ethical and spiritual life has formal expression in and is corroborated by the works of Jesus. The end that he proposes is the same in both. He aims to establish faith in himself not merely as the exponent and interpreter of the truth of God and expression of the power of God, but as the embodiment and final and complete revelation of God to the world. He refuses to be considered apart from the Father, in the energies and activities of his life as well as in his being and self-consciousness. "I speak not of myself:" "the Father that dwelleth in me, he doeth the works." On the one side, the medium of expression and channel of conveyance of the divine power is the human personality of Jesus Christ, and the sphere of operation is that to which the life of man belongs

(87)

and is limited; on the other, the works are such and such only as become him for whom are all things and by whom are all things. They are to be recognized as the doing of the Father, and because of the works themselves he is to be believed.

1. The term that he uses, including his teachings as well as his actions, indicates that he viewed them not as exceptional and extraordinary, but as the natural and fitting expression of his character. To others they seemed to be wonders, miracles, mighty works; to himself there was no wonder, nothing that was not in perfect harmony with his own nature working under the conditions to which he had subjected himself. They bore the same relation to his person, as the life and speech of any man to the quality and faculties of his nature. If there was any miracle, it was in himself and his presence in the midst of this human environment, and not in " his works."

2. At times, viewing his life in its entirety as planned and ordered of his Father, he uses the word in the singular number. " My meat is . . . to finish his work." " I have finished the work thou gavest me to do." All the single and distinct exercises of his power were only so many parts of a complete purpose which he was to accomplish.

3. His work and his works were such and such only as the Father gave him to do. They did not originate with the occasions that called them forth; rather, the occasions were prepared for the working. "Neither hath this man sinned, nor his parents, that he was born blind; but that the works of God should be made manifest in him." Nor did they take their impulse from the affections of his human nature or the solicitations of human need. The affections themselves were but the outcome—the translation into human forms of expression—of divine qualities, divine love and righteousness, directed upon the subjects of the eternal thought of the Father and objects of his infinite solicitude and care. It is impossible to find terms to convey more explicitly, directly, and fully the divine origin and meaning of all that he did than those which he used. "The will of him that sent me." "His work." "The works that the Father hath given me." "The Son can do nothing of himself, but what he seeth the Father do: for what things soever *he* doeth, these also doeth the Son likewise. For the Father loveth the Son, and showeth him all things that himself doeth." It is only as he looks into the mind and will of the Father, and is continuously recipient of his ceaseless, inexhaustible energy that he does his work.

His whole life in its fullness, and each part of it, active or passive, outward or inward, are referred to the same intimate, unbroken, divine relation, and the perfect intercommunion between the Father and the Son. What he seeth—as he only can see " who is in the bosom of the Father "—the Father doing, he doeth.

4. His work was the continuation to its completion of the work of his Father. " My Father worketh hitherto, and I work." " The works that the Father hath given me that I should finish them —the very works that I am doing." To bring to completion, to perfect the work that has been going on through the ages was the business of his incarnate life. The great purpose that had had its first announcement in creation, was declared in the order and movement of the worlds—the κοσμος—was expressed under providential direction in the historic development of the race, and was spoken out in divers portions and in divers manners by the prophets, was to find its fulfillment and final disclosure in the life, speech, labors, and sufferings of the Son of Man. " I have finished the work thou gavest me to do." Beyond this nothing remained but to interpret that life to the ages to come, and to gather up and conserve its results.

5. His life and work were to find their consummate result, first in the offer of salvation to all men, according to his own interpretation of his sufferings and resurrection given by St. Luke, "Thus it behooved Christ to suffer and to rise from the dead: . . . and that repentance and remission of sins should be preached in his name among all nations;" and second, in the revelation of the salvation in the last day, according to the words of the apostle Peter, or in his own language, when "the Son of man shall come in the glory of his Father with his angels, and . . . reward every man according to his works."

For more explicit understanding of their character and purpose it may be best to take account, first, of his work as a whole, and then of his works in relation to the whole and himself. First, his entire work, if in pursuance and completion of the divine purpose and plan, must give to the world,

1. The revelation of God in its fullness. By reason of his personal relation to the Father, he claims the exclusive right and power to declare God. The divine nature, God as God, has never become the subject of direct knowledge to men. Various manifestations had been made under manifold forms and symbols; and from the works of

creation and utterances through the prophets, men
had come to partial knowledge, but never to the
immediate perception of God. "No man hath
seen God at any time; the only begotten Son,
which is in the bosom of the Father, he hath declared him." That directness and fullness of
vision belongs only to him who is of God. He
does not fail to make his disciples know that
such a revelation of God is not possible except
upon conditions of personal attachment and obedience to himself. Whatever discoveries men
may make by natural reason through the things
that are made and by prophetic teachings, they
cannot come to the higher and complete knowledge of God without the manifestation of the Son;
and this is the exclusive right of them that love
him and keep his commandments. "He that
loveth me shall be loved of my Father, and I will
love him, and will manifest myself to him." To
all such he says: "He that hath seen me hath seen
the Father." When to this he adds to the promise of the Comforter—Advocate—whom he would
send from the Father, the Spirit of truth which
proceedeth from the Father, who should testify of
him, who should take the things that were his and
show them to his disciples, it is evident that he intended to exhaust the possibilities of the revelation

of God and to make it all dependent absolutely upon himself. His person was the radiant center from which the effulgence of the glory of the Father should proceed, and only as the Spirit of truth should testify of him could he make men to know of God. "All things that the Father hath are mine: therefore said I, that he shall take of mine, and shall show it unto you."

It was not intended by our Lord to disavow or undervalue that manifestation of God in men, and understanding of the eternal power and Godhead, by the things that are made which St. Paul affirms, nor to depreciate the Hebraic revelations of him. These were the foundations upon which he built. If they had not been already furnished to his hand, he would have been constrained to set them forth first. For the conception of the eternal power and Godhead is the logical and necessary antecedent in thought and consciousness to the final revelation of God in Christ—God the Father, Son, and Spirit. Hence he not only assumes the truthfulness and reality of these former revelations, but appeals to them in confirmation of his own. The God of Abraham, of Isaac, and of Jacob is the God with whom he identifies himself and whose purpose and power he exemplifies and fulfills. The God of the prophets of whom it is said, "All thy children shall be taught of God," is the God whose teaching brings men to him.

There is a tacit admission of a true recognition of God among the Gentiles when he gives assurance that from the north and the south, from the east and the west, they shall come and sit down in the kingdom of God. The ethical and practical value of these revelations is beyond all reckoning. Perverted, abused, and discarded as they so largely were, they yet furnished the only available measure of men's worth, the only ethical standard remaining among men, and the only sufficient incentive and impulse to higher and truer living. At the same time the intimations of immortality were intimately and inseparably bound up with these conceptions of the true God—for God is not the God of the dead, but of the living. The mysterious Melchizedek, whose dim figure passes across the stage of patriarchal history, and Abram, the Chaldean, who was called of God to go to a strange land and obeyed, are early instances of the possibilities of human nature under the urgency of a divine enlightenment; while the long line of priests and prophets and the whole body of Israelitish history give no uncertain proof of the ethical and spiritual elevation attained through such knowledge of God and communion with him.

Fully conceding all this, our Lord gathers into his own person all the ethical value and spiritual potency of the prior manifestations and enhances them beyond measure by disclosures of the interior relations of the Godhead and the transfer of those relations, with all their energies of righteousness, love, and fellowship, to the sphere of human life. He became the embodiment and expression not only of the ancient conception of God, but of the interior activities and affections, all the personal characters of the Godhead brought into fellowship with our nature and expended in its interest. For " in him dwelleth all the fullness of the Godhead bodily, and ye are complete in him."

According to these declarations the measure of any man's knowledge of God is determined by his relation to the Son. Greater than any that had been born of woman was John the Baptist, because his eyes had looked upon, and he had, as taught of God, recognized Jesus as the Son of God. The utterance was more distinct than Abraham's call; the vision more resplendent than the glory shown to Moses. The outlines of that diviner form that had never gladdened the eyes of prophets and kings had passed before him, and upon his ear had fallen the voice from the divided heavens that proclaimed the presence among men of God's beloved Son. No man ever looked with honest eyes and pure heart upon that form without some consciousness of its transforming power, and every recorded word of John shows how he who was sounding and searching the hearts of all men was himself stirred to the lowest depths of his being by conscious and immediate intercourse with the Son of the Most High God. But he that is least in the kingdom of God is greater than John. For to the least of them that love him the word is sure: "He that loveth me shall be loved of my Father, and I will love him, and will manifest myself to him, . . . And my Father will love him, and we will come unto him, and make our abode with him." It is not God only as known to the fathers, but God as the Father revealed in the Son and through the Spirit, and so brought into vital, personal, loving, righteous relation to the heart, conscience, and life of men who love him.

Thus it came to pass that Philip and men like him who had known God had the hunger of their hearts stirred when Jesus brought him before them in their new and higher form, and could not be content without the vision of the Father. "Show

. us the Father, and it sufficeth us." Hence, too, it
is that wherever Christ is preached neither the
Gentile conception, nor the Hebraic revelation sat-
isfies the heart of men. The old petition is repeated: " Show us the Father." The Son is come
into the midst of us, identified himself with us,
touched our inmost being, quickened, intensified
it. Near as he is to us, let us know that Father,
from whom come forth this diviner humanity, these
deeper, tenderer affections, this beauty of holiness
—let us know whom he calls Father; show him
to us, that we may share in the power and
blessedness of such communion. The cry only
shows that now and then our eyes are holden that
we should not know him. To see the Son is to see
the Father, whether he come in the lowliness of
human flesh, in the garments of poverty, with the
shame and sorrow of the cross, or in glow and
splendor of his triumph and the transcendent glory
of his regal life as John in Patmos saw him.
"And every one that seeth the Son and believeth
on him, may have everlasting life."

2. With the revelation of God, Jesus Christ
brought the revelation of man.

(1) By the communion with God essential to
the knowledge of him the dignity, the worth, and
the possibilities of human nature are unmistakably

affirmed. The conscious possession and use of faculties through which he apprehends the Maker and Lord of all things, and searches out his works, discovering his purpose and coming into sympathy with his plans, declares his participation in measure in the divine nature, and puts him above the level of mere plastic, unresponsive material. In so far as he can understand and appreciate his will and methods he has personal interest in the Creator and Ruler of all; and in the sphere of his own energies, where he appropriates, directs, it may be modifies, processes that have their origin and their end in the mind of God, he becomes an active participant in divine plans and movements—a worker " together with God.'" The extent of his personal influence and the effect that he may produce upon final issues depend upon the fullness of his understanding of God, and the completeness of his conformity to the purpose and methods of God. The Son of Man gave the supreme instance of the possibilities of our nature, in his incarnate career, and gave promise to them that believe on him of enhanced power and imperial life as the result of his own release from the restrictions of the flesh and return to the seat of the Godhead. " The works that I do shall he do also; and greater works than these shall he do; because I go unto

my Father." "He that overcometh" shall "sit
with me in my throne." Such a revelation bears
with it the assurance, quickens the consciousness
of immortality. The idea of death—of final extinction—is impossible to the man who knows God
and is conscious of fellowship and coöperation and
coagency with him. The inner truth of our Lord's
words, "God is not the God of the dead, but of
the living," becomes essential in his experience.
To this answers the declaration of the Father's
will "that every one which seeth the Son, and believeth on him"—the full process of revelation—
"may have eternal life; and I will raise him up at
the last day"—the consciousness of indestructible
life guaranteed by the resurrection at the last day.

(2) By this revelation the ethical relations—*i. e.*,
all the living relations—of men are determined.

Jesus Christ by revealing the Father has not
changed the quality of moral rectitude nor put it
upon other grounds than were before set forth.
He did not come to destroy, but to fulfill. He did
give definiteness to the meaning of righteousness
and far wider scope to its application as a principle and power in men. For with utmost explicit-
ness and directness he proclaims the righteousness
of God as alone true, and the only standard by
which the relations of men are to be tried. Not

undervaluing the legal enactment, nor discarding the ceremonial requirement in their rightful use, he refuses to admit them as final limitations of obligation, and will not refer to them as the final exponents of rectitude. He first enters the regions of human nature where God and man are brought together, and in the light of the divine relationship sets forth the qualities upon which real righteousness must be founded. It is not simply the relation of man to man that is to be established, but first, and as indispensable to the other, the relation of man to God. It is not any kingdom of this world that is imaged forth in his word and life; it is the kingdom of God.

Further, this righteous relation between God and man is determined not by the proclivities, needs, and possibilities of the inferior party, but by the attributes and possible revealments of the Most High. From his way of speaking we might suppose that he sees righteousness in its last analysis to belong to the interior life of the Godhead and to grow out of the distinctions therein. The Son calls upon him as the " righteous Father," proclaiming righteousness as the dominant factor in the Father's dealing with himself; and in his transactions with the Father as the Advocate for men the Son is Jesus Christ the righteous. Bringing it thus out of the depths of the Godhead, and determining upon it all the relations between God and man, and, at the same time, in his own person declaring the extent and intimacy of those relations, he has given an ethical, a divine quality to life unknown before. In the liturgy and service and casuistry of life the scribe and the Pharisee, rabbi and priest are swept aside, and conscience and heart are laid "naked and open before the eyes of him with whom we have to do." In the precincts of the household the law of coarse concessions to the hardness of imbruted nature and of license to the untamed passions of unclean souls is abolished, and return to the simplicity, purity, and sweetness of the divine beginnings demanded. "In the beginning it was not so" is his answer to Pharisaic appeal to Moses's law. Every grade and station of life, and all its transactions, are brought into the same divine light and subjected to the same scrutiny. The law of God's righteousness is universal and inexorable. "Every plant which my heavenly Father hath not planted, shall be rooted up." "Be ye perfect, even as your Father in heaven is perfect."

3. The work of the Son of God is further characterized as redemptive. In every way he keeps this purpose before the minds of men. The

fact of the sin of the world is set over against the righteousness of God, as declared by him and illustrated in his own person. The power of sin is exemplified in the reception and treatment of himself, even when he is most lavish in the expenditure of his resources for the good of men. The evil and danger of sin are proclaimed in terms whose solemn and awful import even to-day makes the hearts of men fail them for fear, and find their last meaning only in fathomless abysses of the outer darkness, into which he, with all his tenderness, compassion, and longing for men, sends no faintest ray of hope. It was this above all else that brought about the incarnation. Whether in the process of revelation he would have assumed our nature had there been no sin; whether, apart from the existence and effect of sin, such form of manifestation of God would have been needed, it is vain to inquire. We can only conjecture and speculate in this region of thought. If any advantage is ever to be gained from answer to the inquiry, we may safely relegate it to the category of the things to be revealed in higher and clearer light. What we know not now we shall know hereafter. It is enough for us now that he identifies revelation and redemption, proclaims it to be the end of his coming to take away sin, and explains

his life at the last by its relation to repentance and
remission of sins.

(1) First of all he completes the revelation of
sin. Here, as in every other line, he brings to
perfection that which had in divers degrees and
divers manners been done before. By the law was
the knowledge of sin. But the law made nothing
perfect. He came to fulfill—to fill out, to complete the work of the law. Limited in its range by
the conditions under which it was given and the
sphere in which it was operative, the law offered
only the shadow of good things to come, and not
the very image of the things. Its meaning and
effect could not pass beyond the worship embodied in the ceremonial institute which gave it expression. It is an old saying, and true, that man
never rises higher than his worship. Here were
ordinances of service and a cosmic sanctuary
and all the material symbols pertaining thereto,
the copies of things in the heavens. There was
an inner shrine to which only the high priest
dared approach, suggestive of more and better
than was open to the mind and conscience of the
people. However far-reaching the suggestion
might be, the actual effect upon the understanding
and the ethical faculty was limited by the outward
and earthly form of the service and by the media-

tion of it through men who were given to death.
The measurement of sin by quantity and quality
of sacrifice was fatal to its deeper spiritual appreciation, a legal defect remedied only in part by
the fact that many transgressions more immediately affecting the relations of men to God were
left wholly without sacrificial remedy, and by
the further fact that prophecy with its diviner
insight and further reach of authority was super-
imposed upon the law. It was prophecy that
searched the conscience of David and elicited the
confession: "I have sinned against the Lord."
It was prophecy alone that dared to say: "The
Lord also hath put away thy sin." No priest in
Israel would have provided sacrifice or proffered
forgiveness for such offense.

The very energy with which the law wrought
its way into all the details of life, and sought by
specific enactment to bring within its scope every
possible condition and line of endeavor, was confession of its weakness; and at the same time, as
with the growth of the centuries, life became more
complex and the application of law more difficult,
it inevitably degenerated into Rabbinism, and became a yoke which, in apostolic language, "neither our fathers nor we were able to bear." Under the influence of this tendency sin became a

hopeless perplexity and life an intolerable burden. There were, of course, as already intimated, higher views of man's relation to God, in the light of which the conception of sin was deepened and intensified. The Psalms and the prophets give ample witness to this. Indeed, so intense and thorough was the conviction of sin expressed in them that the Church of to-day can find no truer or better terms in which to offer her confession and make her supplication. But even this fuller utterance must be interpreted by the conditions of the times, and measured as to its import by their conceptions of the God made known to them. Its deepest meaning is declared to us only when we bring it into the intense light of the final revelation of God made in his Son. For to the prophets who searched what the Spirit of Christ in them did signify it was revealed that " not unto themselves, but unto us they did minister."

Jesus Christ made full use of the law and the prophets, in their proper application, for the conviction of sin. He sends the leper—the type and open expression to the Jew of the effect of sin—to the priest to offer for his cleansing as the law required, and thus made legal ordinances obligatory upon them that were under the law. He bade the people observe what the scribes and

Pharisees commanded, because they sat in Moses's seat. He tested the conscience and life of the anxious young ruler by the commandments, and time and again quoted the words of the prophet Isaiah to convince the people of sin and to rebuke them. But he gave the law a more profound meaning than priest or rabbi ever knew, and, transcending its preceptive form into living force and discarding the measurements and applications of the visible sanctuary, sent it with its divine energy and sanction into the most secret recesses of the soul, searching the very thoughts and intents of the heart. He summed up all prophecy in the pregnant words of Isaiah which he read in the synagogue at Nazareth, and applied it to himself, "This day is this scripture fulfilled in your ears," and thenceforth charged men with sin because they believed not on him, and declared that without faith in him there was no deliverance from sin possible. "If ye believe not that I am he, ye shall die in your sins."

Nor does he content himself with words. The divine authority with which he speaks, the blameless holiness of his life, and the might of his working compel the recognition in his person of a standard of life and character to which all legal estimates must yield, and before which the righteousness of the law, exemplified in Simon, who had never "eaten anything common or unclean," shrinks with the confession of sin, and the gross licentiousness of the woman that was a sinner melts away into repentant tears. Under the light of the divine relations set forth in him, the old conceptions of sin appear entirely inadequate and are merged and lost in the enormity of the one supreme offense of rejecting him. "If I had not come and spoken unto them, . . . if I had not done among them the works which none other man did, they had not had sin: but now have they both seen and hated both me and my Father." Beyond this the estimate of sin could not go. Divine authority resisted, divine righteousness rejected, divine love insulted—the very foundations of the order of the worlds and of human hope subverted in the refusal to believe and receive him whom the Father hath sent into the world. So rooted has this estimate become in the conscience of the world, that until to-day, in spite of equivocations and sentimental attempts to excuse or mitigate it, the one supreme, typical sin in the world's history is the treachery of Judas —the last possibility of wrong done to the Son of God. The heart echoes the words of the Christ, "It were better for him that he had never been born," and shudders at the awful significance of the apostle's saying that " he went to his own place."

(2) But " God sent not his Son into the world to condemn the world, but that the world through him might be saved." It was not only that he might make sin fully known and show its exceeding sinfulness, but that he might provide for and offer remission of sins and deliverance from its power. The Son of Man came to seek and to save that which was lost. It is here that the wonder and the power of his life appear. Everything else falls into the commonplace when compared with the marvelous achievement of taking away the sin of the world—taking it away from the relations between God and men, and renewing and transforming the moral and spiritual nature of men.

It may be well here to utter a caution against the indifference to and depreciation of this side of our Lord's work, characteristic of some phases of thought, and common to men whose sense of sin is blunted and whose conceptions of sin are low and narrow. To them it seems an easy thing for God to forgive sin—a prompting of his loving, kindly, compassionate nature, to which he can freely yield himself, as he is without responsibility to any. We may not go far into the nature of God, nor inquire too curiously into the moral qualities and relations essential to him, and which control all his affections toward and his transactions with his intelligent creatures. We know only so much as he has revealed and as finds response in our self-consciousness and ethical sense. So much is certain: that this life of the Son of God, thrown with all its resplendent characters and possibilities of power and endurance into the midst of men—the most startling and amazing phenomenon upon which the world has ever looked—was absolutely devoted to this one thing; and the only reason of his death which he gave was that it was essential to the remission of sins. "This is my blood of the new testament, which is shed for many for the remission of sins."

In attempting to express more fully his own view of this side of his work we are guarded against a too bold and aggressive statement of any definite theory by the reserve of our Lord's speech and the entire absence of anything like a formal explanation of the principles involved in redemption. Yet we are constrained by the demands of faith and emboldened by apostolic example to ascertain and assert the great facts—not only historic, within time, but eternal—which fur-

nish the ground of atonement, and give cogency
to its appeal to the higher spiritual nature in man.
These facts were expressed in his person and life,
rather than formulated and logically connected
with the great result to be achieved. A pregnant
sentence now and then offers us a glimpse into
his own consciousness, and helps us to interpret
from within the purpose and work of a life that
from without could find no sufficient explanation.
By reference to such utterances we may be able
to signalize the leading essential facts, and perhaps shall find in them the best answer to the cav-
ils that have been flung at the supreme truth of
the gospel, the only sufficient provision for human
want, and the ground and source of hope for the
world.

1. Jesus Christ assumes that of right and by
personal authority he only, in all the universe, can
undertake and accomplish the redemption of men
and the rectification of the disorder in the universe
occasioned by sin. It is a business into which
none other can intrude, and for which no other is
competent.

2. This right and power he refers to his own
eternal relations with God and his consequent,
original, and indefeasible relations with men and
with the entire creation. The oft-repeated affir-

mations in manifold form of the glory that he had
with the Father before the world was are not intended simply to declare the majesty of his person
and enhance the greatness of his sacrifice and
add luster to the crown of his achievement, but
rather to show in these original relations the
ground and reason of his undertaking, to indicate
the fullness of his power and the sufficiency of his
authority to intervene in human affairs.   St. Paul
states the case with more than philosophical pre-
cision and in logical order when he writes to the
Colossians of " the Son of his love; in whom we
have our redemption, the forgiveness of our sins:
who is the image of the invisible God, the firstborn of all creation; for in him were all things
created, in the heavens and upon the earth, things
visible and things invisible, whether thrones or
dominions or principalities or powers; all things
have been created through him, and unto him; and
he is before all things, and in him all things consist.
And he is the head of the body, the church; who
is the beginning, the firstborn from the dead;
that in all things he might have the preëminence."   With fuller statement on the side of the
process of incarnation the Gospel of John affirms
the same relations and their significance.   The
intimation of his prerogative is given by our Lord

in the parable of the husbandman: " They will reverence my Son." " This is the heir; come, let us kill him, and the inheritance shall be ours." No less distinct is the teaching of the Epistle to the Hebrews: " God hath spoken to us by his Son, whom he appointed heir of all things, through whom also he made the worlds; who being the effulgence of his glory and the very image of his substance, and upholding all things by the word of his power, when he had made purification of sins, sat down on the right hand of the majesty on high." It matters little whether the phrase " by himself" be retained, or, as in the Revised Version, omitted. The sense is unchanged. The Son, Heir of all things and Creator of the worlds, alone has authority to come in and take control of human affairs. The effulgence of the glory of God alone can displace the darkness of sin. The power of him who upholds all things by his word is alone sufficient to "take away the sin of the world." The interference of another in this sphere of his exclusive relations and absolute right and power would be an intrusion, an impertinence, an invasion of divine prerogatives. When the chief of the apostles in his ignorant amazement presumed to touch, however lightly, with mere suggestion of human wisdom these " things that be of God," the stern repulse, "Get thee behind me, Satan," warned him off from this region into which only the daring effrontery of the prince of darkness would venture, to his own shame and discomforture.

It is needful to keep this feature of revelation clearly before us. For the questions that arise upon the discussion of the atonement are nearly all framed upon the view of human relations and the analogies that they seem to furnish to the great transaction. There are no analogies possible in the visible and natural relations of men to this event. It is as absolutely unique and without precedent and parallel as the person of the Son of God. Incidents in human life and ceremonial ordainments may furnish types and shadows of partial phases of the work of redemption, and give hint to men of deeper meanings and broader purpose than they could express; but it was a mystery hidden from the ages and made known only when God sent "his own Son in the likeness of sinful flesh." It had its beginning in the interior life of the Godhead in the relations between the Father, who is the Fountain and Source of all being, and the Son, through whom all things were made and in whom all things consist, and who answers to the Father as the only Mediator for all

8

things. We grope our way with dim and uncertain vision when we enter these regions of divine
life. We cannot sound these abysses. But we
surely do not abate the reverence due to him who
dwells in light that no man can approach unto,
when we fling some rays from the face of his Son
upon the inscrutable· mystery, and set forth the
redemption by Jesus Christ as having its roots
within the Godhead, in the eternal relations between the Father and the Son.

Has not our gospel suffered by being drawn too
far down into the region of mere human thought
and visible relations? It is a divine thing to lift
human associations and sympathies to the heavenly places and shape them, after their true and
original intent, into reflections of divine relations.
We were made at the first after the likeness and
image of God. But to take our notions of divine
rule ·from the conventions and institutions of this ·
world, to frame the laws of the kingdom of heav-
en in agreement with our sociological science, to
bring the righteousness of God into harmony with
results drawn from *data* of ethics gathered from
the manifold capricious forms and experiences of
the visible sensuous life and to test the principles
of divine life and administration by the abstrae-
tions of human intellect is surely to reverse the

true order and incur the reproach, "Thou thoughtest that I was altogether such an one as thyself." It should be ours to maintain the lofty tone of the divine testimonies, and keep reverently in mind that our Christ " was in the beginning with God," " the Lamb slain from the foundation of the world," and that we were "chosen in him before the foundation of the world," and cannot take our understanding of the things of God from the wisdom of this world, or of the princes of this world, in whatever department they may have rule.

The relations of the Son to men also date back to eternal beginnings. He is the " firstborn of all creation," and " in him all things consist." On the one side, as the image of the invisible God receiving into himself all the fullness of divine life, he manifests it in the making and holding together in himself of all things, and expresses it in his personal relations to intelligent creatures; on the other, as the only sufficient and rightful representative of the worlds, he answers for them to the Father. It is in virtue of all this that he distinguishes between himself and all other men. Greater than Solomon, greater than Jonah, setting his " I say unto you " above the word of prophet and lawgiver, and denouncing a heavier condemnation than had fallen upon Tyre and Sidon, Sodom and Gomorrah, against the cities that had refused to give heed to his offer. Profoundly in sympathy with men and a friend of publicans and sinners, he refused to be classed with them. He was made in all things like unto his brethren, yet was separated from sinners and made higher than the heavens. He admits none to share in his functions and in exercise of his authority, uses men only as messengers and witnesses for himself. He extends the scope of his authority and personal relationship through all time and to the uttermost parts of the earth. He is not simply the ideal of human character and life and the most potent factor in human history—the sublimated and sanctified hero and martyr of humanity; he is " the Word become flesh "—the Word in his original rights and relations and with his authority unimpaired sent and coming into the body of our humanity, and exercising his prerogatives through the organs of incarnate life and by the ways of human fellowship. Historically, within the limits of time, he asserts and exercises the powers and rights of his eternal life.

3. The form and manner of this entrance into human history constitute another feature in his redemptive work. In his speech it is characterized

as transfer from the sphere of the Godhead to the limited region of the temporal life. "I proceeded forth and came from God." "The Father sent me." It is a form of speech which finds its best interpretation in the process described by St. Paul: "Being in the form of God, he thought it not a thing to be grasped after to be equal with God, but emptied himself, taking the form of a servant, being made in the likeness of men." In the freer rendering of a Bampton lecturer, "He was essentially in the form of God, so that it was no invasion of the divine to claim equality with God; and yet he laid this aside and put on the form of our human servitude." It is the Word become flesh, the conjunction of his entire and absolute authority over all things with servitude and sacrifice, the restriction of his power to the limits prescribed by human weakness and its use through the organic forms and according to the divine order of human life.

It is in this first movement of descent that the principle and power of redemption appear, to be carried forward in the development of his incarnate life until they culminate in the passion and the cross. The question so often put, "Is it righteous that the innocent be made to suffer for the guilty?" has no pertinence here. It belongs only to the sphere of human life and relations, and as far as it has any application to the human life of the Son of God it has its answer in the unqualified condemnation pronounced by the gospel and the world upon all who were in any degree implicated in his death. Caiaphas is not exonerated because he prophesied unconsciously the great fact of atonement by Jesus Christ, any more than Pilate who judged him, or Judas who betrayed him. "Ye with wicked hands have crucified and slain him." God and man concur in executing vengeance against those who betrayed and shed innocent blood. Judas and Jerusalem are witnesses. But a broader relation and a higher righteousness than the terms of individual human life can cover are involved here. He was delivered by the determinate counsel and foreknowledge of God. In his own language, he was "sent of God, of the Father." Himself privy to the counsel and participant in the transaction, he came out from the Godhead to reassert his own and his Father's right and righteousness, and recover the world from the power and effect of sin. It does not concern us how sin had its beginning, or why he suffered it even in its inception. It is enough to be assured that this invasion of divine right and enemy of all righteousness could not be allowed to

maintain its hold forever upon the world which the
Son of God claimed as his own.   He came to assert his right; he came as the Word made flesh.
His first, supreme work was "in the likeness
of sinful flesh, and on account of sin, to condemn sin in the flesh." He was made under law, in
form of a servant, and by absolute devotion to his
Father's will declared and illustrated the divine
righteousness which was fatal to sin.   As a mere
unit in the teeming multitudes of the race, an individual with exceptional and extraordinary gifts and
qualities of character he might have had influence
proportioned to his human worth and power.   It
is not possible to say how far this might have
reached.   Mere human character at its best is
great beyond expression, and touches life over
vast areas and along immeasurable tracts of time.
Of the first recorded instance it is still, after all
these ages of growth, change, revolution, written
and written truly: "He being dead yet speaketh."
But more than mere human influence is in contemplation here.   The divine righteousness essential to
the life of the Godhead and to the relations and
transactions between God and the world is vindicated and exhibited.   More than the worth and
power of an individual life is required.

A moment may well be given here to the consid-

eration of an element that has been abstractly and
theologically discussed, but as a vital fact and
essential to redemption has hardly been sufficiently taken into account. Our human nature is not
made up of a multitude of separate, disconnected
units. It is a vast organic whole, each part in vital connection with every other. We cannot set
aside individual character and responsibility.
There is in each of us the isolation of an awful
solitude into which no other can intrude. But it
is an inevitable condition that no man liveth or
dieth to himself. His character is formed in association with others, and his destiny determined
largely by the terms of his related life. In the
narrow range of our common life, we hardly need
to be reminded of it. In the fields of thought and
action, we own our indebtedness for much the
largest part of what we are and hope to become to
the material and opportunities furnished by ever-
enlarging circles of life. Where sympathy and affection are engaged the sense of oneness with other life becomes more intense, and the impressions
in consciousness and character more deep and
abiding. Farther reaching than this is the law that
binds us through ever multiplying and divergent
lines to the generations of the past, so that by
heredity and transmitted agencies and institutions,

by history and tradition, we have been made what we are. We are the product of hundreds of generations, and shall in turn contribute to the building up of the coming world and to the shaping of its destiny. Of those gone before us it is said: "They without us shall not be made perfect." This, which is true in science and in the common life of this world, is more profoundly true of the higher moral and spiritual realm to which men belong. Here the "unity of nature" is affirmed with a completeness unknown amidst the divisive tendencies of the fleshly life. A divine purpose and order including all things, community of life proceeding from the same divine source, interdependence, affection, sympathy, are indicated in the body with its one head and many members, "every one members one of another." Its final realization will be after the pattern of the divine unity—as "Thou, Father, art in me, and I in thee, that they also may be one in us."

Into this body of our humanity, as its rightful Head and in closer and more vital connection with it as a whole, and with every member of it, than any other could be, Jesus Christ came.

It is with this body as a whole that God first deals. Whatever may be the claims of the individual conscience and the needs of the individual

man—and these are never forgotten—the work of
Christ is for the world, and his relations as the
"word made flesh" are with the world. The
world is conceived of as wrought upon by man,
who is the crown and lord of it all, involving it in
his disorder and degradation. "God so loved the
world," "sent his Son into the world," "I am
the light of the world," and many such like sayings, as well as the commission and provision for
the final process of gathering in the world, point to
the true purpose of God. Creation culminates in
humanity, and humanity culminates in Jesus.
Christ, as come in the flesh, is the ideal which God
had in view in the process of creation. So then
in the beginning the race as a whole was had in
contemplation in the creation by Jesus Christ, and
at the last the race is to be brought into oneness,
and all things gathered together in one—in Jesus
Christ.

These suggestions indicate the nature of the
work of Jesus Christ in redemption: 1. He as Head,
Creator, in whom all things consist, is in vital relation to the world of mankind, and every individual
of the race is in intimate connection with him. 2.
His entrance into our flesh puts him in the same
relation to God as the world into which he comes:
made of a woman, made under the law, bound up

with the body of mankind, subject to its conditions.
3. As required by these conditions, he fulfills all
righteousness, does the work of a servant, doing
not his own will, but the will of Him that sent him.
4. He endures the penalty fallen upon the race.
"Sin entered into the world, and death by sin; and
so death passed upon all men, for that all have
sinned." In his personal right he was exempt;
in his identification of himself with humanity he
claimed no exemption. He held himself answer-
able to the Father for the world which owed its being to him. He was made sin for us who knew no
sin. 5. Finally by his resurrection he vindicated
the power of personal righteousness and sent forth
into the world the new life for the recovery of men.
From beginning to end of the incarnate career, under the burden of servitude, in presence of human
scorn, hate and treachery, through all the torture
of the garden and the cross he asserts his divine
authority, puts himself at the head of mankind,
and declares his very presence among men, his
work and his sufferings, to be voluntary and for the
world's salvation, and vindicates his claims by the
resurrection. Witness his word, " I lay down my
life of myself; no man taketh it from me. I lay
it down of myself and I take it again;" his rebuke of his disciples, " I could presently call upon

my Father, and he would send me twelve legions
of angels;" his attitude of independence before
Pilate, "Thou couldst have no power over me at
all except it were given thee from above."

Thus in his person we have the righteousness of
God manifested, remission of sins declared, and as
mediating and reconciling these otherwise irrecon-
cilable factors, the propitiation.   By these he finished the work given him to do.

But little needs to be said of his works.   They
are but illustrations in detail of his work as a whole.
The leading feature in them is that indicated by
the most frequent word used for them, " signs."
They were intended to be only intimations and
suggestions of the truth and power that lay behind
them, and, like his parables, to induce men to inquire for and into the thing signified.   In this view
they were tests of character.   In some, as Peter
at the draught of fishes, they quickened the inner
sense and brought out the confession of sin.   Some
regarded them only as an extraordinary provision
for the natural wants of men, and sought him not
because they saw the signs, but because they " did
eat of the loaves, and were filled."   No doubt they
thought that with a leader who could care for his
fellows after this sort, Jewish hopes might soon be
realized and the yoke of hated Rome be broken

off. Others still, in their malignity and envy, could see in them only the working of demoniac powers, and charged his miracles to the account of Beelzebub, the prince of devils. In all cases the reception and use of them fairly determined the mind of the man toward Christ, and his fitness for the kingdom of God. Ten lepers were cleansed, and none returned to give thanks to God but the Samaritan. " Where were the nine? "

Looking at them from another point of view, they are assertions of his authority over all things. In this sense, too, they have value as signs. No such power over winds and seas, earth and air, and all things therein, could be lodged in any but the rightful Lord of men. " Whether is easier to say, Thy sins be forgiven thee; or to say, Arise, and walk? " But apart from this significance they are in entire keeping with the attitude which he took invariably toward all men and all things. He was here as the heir, sent by the Father to assert his rights and authority, and whenever need arose or occasion offered he did so. He did not heal all the sick, nor raise all the dead, nor cleanse all the lepers. When he ascended, the sum of the world's suffering and sorrow was scarcely perceptibly less than when he came among men. But the keynote to the new

song had been given. Whenever leper, lame,
blind, sick, or dead was brought before him in
sincere recognition of his authority, he declared
his power. Devils recognized it. He would do
nothing for himself, but anything, everything for
them that believed in him. Henceforth the world
may know that all power in heaven and earth,
even to the remission of sins, is given to him.

In another view they were in confirmation of
his claims, attestations of the divinity of his person. So the text. They are the normal and inevitable expressions of his character. The wonder in relation to them is the reserve which char-
acterizes them. In the sweep of his power he
might have gone through Judea and Palestine,
banishing plague and pestilence, breaking up the
graves and abolishing cemeteries, bringing comfort and joy to the bereaved homes and hearts of
the multitudes. But he restricts himself to the
few who can answer affirmatively: "Believest
thou that I am able to do this?" In every instance
he tells what he is by what he does. Whether
for help and healing—tribute to be paid, and multitudes to be fed—or for judgment, as on the bar-
ren fig tree, he makes men know that he is but exercising his native right. The wonder is not in
what he does, but in what he is and that he is here.

Finally, his works express the mind and heart of God to men. They are the things that the Father is doing. Power, compassion, helpfulness, judgment—in all alike, and in each instance he simply declares how the Father thinks and feels. It is the veritable revelation of God in human action and sympathy.

He is the same yesterday and to-day and forever. To find what is the mind of God toward you and the world of the present, search for the dealings of his Son with men. The sins are the same, the weakness and the woe, and the graves are still close sealed; but the Son of Man, the Son of God, brightness of the glory of God, is in power, and compassion the same, and only waits until the world shall own him, to wipe away all tears and open all graves.

LECTURE IV.

THE WITNESS OF THE SCRIPTURES.

9

IV.

"Search the Scriptures; for in them ye think ye have eternal life: and they are they which testify of me. And ye will not come to me, that ye might have life." John v. 39, 40.

WHETHER read in the imperative or, with the Revised Version, in the indicative, the words point the Jews to the futility of their search and rebuke their failure to take true direction from the Scriptures. They expected to obtain eternal life. But the Scriptures told them of Christ. If they had believed and been obedient to them, they would have known the Christ, and coming to him would have had life. It is clear that our Lord intended to refer his claims to the testimony of the Scriptures, those Scriptures which we know as the Old Testament. The language is too plain to be misunderstood. But it has ample support from the appeals to Moses and the prophets, the quotations from them in his teachings and in the special instruction which he gave his disciples in the Scriptures concerning himself. "Beginning at Moses and all the prophets, he expounded" to the two disciples on the way to Emmaus "in all the

(131)

Scriptures the things concerning himself;" and in his last hours with them, " Then opened he their understanding, that they might understand the Scriptures, and said unto them, Thus it is written, and thus it behooved Christ to suffer, and to rise from the dead." In pursuance of his method the apostles reasoned with Jews and Gentiles out of the Scriptures, showing that Jesus was the Christ.

As our Lord distinctly declined to rest his claims upon mere human testimony, even such as John's, he evidently intended to set the Scriptures apart and assign to them a value attaching to no other records as authoritative and divine. He calls them the word of God, and affirms their perpetual significance and obligation.

The scope and limits of this lecture do not admit of a discussion of the questions raised by this appeal. We have only to state the conclusions to which we are shut up by the use made of the Scriptures by our Lord and his apostles.

1. The stability and integrity of our gospel are bound up with the inspiration and divine authority of the Old Testament. We are " built upon the foundation of the apostles and prophets, Jesus Christ himself being the chief corner stone." Apostolic and prophetic teaching unite and are held together in Jesus Christ. They do not sim-

ply constitute separate parts, either of which may be removed without danger to the other. They are inseparably combined. Blot out from the New Testament the features which identify it with the Old, and little will be left that is worth contending for. Take away the material in history, thought, worship, and experience drawn from the Old Testament, and you destroy the validity of our Lord's appeal and the argument of apostolic preaching. No concessions to the power and purity of the gospel, no admissions of its ethical value to the world, will avail to sustain it as an isolated and independent institution and agency. By its own terms it is committed to such intimate and vital relationship to the Old Scriptures that they stand or fall together.

2. The Scriptures were intended for our learning, for our admonition, "upon whom the ends of the ages are come." They had not only the abiding quality characteristic of many works of genius, but were distinguished from all other literature in that they addressed themselves to the ages to come rather than to their own generations. Like the institutes of the tabernacle, they were but a figure, or parable for the time then present, whose meaning should be fully disclosed only when the way into the holiest of all should be made manifest.

So says the apostle Peter: "The prophets inquired and searched diligently, . . . what, or what manner of time the Spirit of Christ which was in them did signify. . . . Unto whom it was revealed, that not unto themselves, but unto us they did minister the things, that are now reported unto you by them that have preached the gospel unto you."

3. They were the product of a divine influence upon the minds of men, and as such carried with them the authority of divine command and the certainty of divine truth. "All Scripture is given by inspiration of God." The testimony is not substantially altered if the reading of the Revised Version be adopted: "Every scripture inspired of God is also profitable for teaching, for reproof, for correction, for instruction which is in righteousness: that the man of God may be complete, furnished completely unto every good work." For it still affirms inspiration for the class of Scripture referred to, and the writer, in common with his Lord and the other apostles, makes appeal to no other than the Old Testament to instruct in righteousness, and furnish for every good work. To this agree the words of the apostle Peter, when he adduces in proof of the power and coming of our Lord Jesus Christ the "more sure word of prophecy . . .

as unto a light that shineth in a dark place, until the day dawn, and the daystar arise in your heart," and affirms that no prophecy was ever brought by the will of man, "but men spake from God, being moved by the Holy Ghost." In the same way almost every Epistle, as well as the Gospels, Acts of the Apostles, and Apocalypse of John, refers to and uses the ancient Hebrew Scriptures. They are brought forward, not as selected and preserved specimens of the highest and best thought and literature of the nation, nor even as an element in its religious life with a liturgical value and having the sanctity of worship attached to it, but as the authoritative standard of righteousness for the world, the divine revelation of things not seen, and the only promise of hope to all men. The claim is that these books were written by men chosen of God for the purpose and enlightened by the Holy Spirit.

By the terms of our gospel we are more than justified in reading the Old Testament Scriptures in the light of the later history. It is not an unfair or uncritical treatment of them. It is not an attempt to read into them our own later conceptions of what ought to have been, and upon this foundation to frame a system that shall represent human character and destiny and divine righteousness as the world of to-day understands them. That is rather the spirit of those who deny the validity and authority of the record because it is not according to the mind of our time, or would read out of it everything that is not capable of test by the critical standards of this world's wisdom.

We take as our guides, first, the prophets themselves, who accepted the teaching that in coming events they should find the interpretation of the things then spoken and events then occurring; second, of our Lord and his apostles, who re ferred their own work and teaching to divine authority as attested by the prophetic Scriptures, and constantly explained the past by the occurrences of their time; and finally, even that entire class of historical inquirers who seek—and not in vain—the sources and motives of their own age in the antecedent currents of life, and find clearer understanding of the former times in the issues of the present.

We violate no principle of historical criticism when we thus insist upon the unity of revelation and take our understanding of its earlier portions from the final result in which they have combined and culminated. We do, in our treatment of the preparatory history and the older records, hold ourselves under the restraint of the divine caution:

" My thoughts are not your thoughts, neither are
your ways my ways, saith the Lord." It should
therefore be our endeavor to find the divine methods of revelation, especially as taught by Christ,
and trace them in the Scriptures of the Old Testament. The character and meaning of the work
of the Son of God give us the true line of direction
in our inquiry into the purport and final effect of
those Scriptures. According to these we look for
revelation in such degrees and forms as would prepare the way for the final manifestation of God in
his Son, for intimations of redemptive purpose and
its methods that would clearly enough point to the
incarnation and the sacrifice of the Son of God as
their fulfillment, and for divine direction of and interposition in human affairs to the extent necessary to make ready a people prepared for the
Lord.

In the life of Jesus Christ we are ·dealing with
the most momentous event in the history of our
world—an event entirely unique, and holding within itself elements and forces intended to affect the
whole course of human history and to determine
the destinies of all men, and lying quite apart from
the reach of mere human investigation. To
thrust such an event rudely and without preparation into the current of human affairs would have

been to discredit the providential order of movement in the world, to disturb and turn off into irregular and erratic courses the normal processes
of thought, and to fling the minds and lives of
men into the insanities of groundless faith and fa-
natical endeavor. It is hardly conceivable that
the incarnation of the Son of God, and his life,
death, and resurrection, permeated by and satu-
rated with the supernatural quality, should have
made their immediate demand upon the faith and
obedience of men without such full preparation.
Unless there were an abrupt and violent departure
from all his recognized methods of working,
God must have prepared the way for the coming
of his Son by a dispensation heavily charged with
supernatural elements; or, to put the same statement in another form, the foregoing course of human events must have been so evidently directed
of God and have furnished such supernatural
manifestations of his presence as to give ground
and reason for faith in the full and final revelation
in his Son.

It can hardly be doubted that God would provide in some measure such witness to himself
among the Gentiles, and amidst their perversions
of truth, abuses of nature, and idolatries of worship leave some possibilities of the discovery of

better things. Indeed, the records and monu-
ments of history give ample intimation that the
thought of the one God, however dim and uncertain it had come to be, had not utterly died out
from the minds of men, that, as St. Paul charged,
they knew God, though they glorified him not as
God; and the Old Testament Scriptures show that
all the great heathen nations were at some moment
in their life brought into relation, for good or evil,
with the chosen people, and had opportunity to
learn, if they would, the divine meaning of events
clearly outside the range of natural movement—
such as the plagues of Egypt, and the destruction
of Sennacherib's army, the mission of Elisha to
Hazael, and of Jonah to Nineveh—which profoundly affected themselves, and grew out of their
intercourse with Israel.

If we could read the history of the old world in
its completeness, we should surely find that, as old
Theophilus Gale put it, God had provided in his
great temple a " Court of the Gentiles," where
they might learn his will and render him worship.

But while there are in our New Testament oc-
casional references to the interest and intervention
of God in the affairs of the world at large, the
stress of the argument in behalf of the Christ is
laid upon the records of the Old Testament as the

revelation of the purpose of God, and the preparation for the coming of his Son. "They are they," said Christ, "which testify of me."

Assuming the authority of the record, it is our first business to look into the nature and contents of the testimony adduced. The contents are varied. History, law, prophecy, devotion, proverb— all have their place in the series. One general observation applies to them all, which is that they partake of the prophetic quality. We do not hazard much in saying that from the point of view of our Scriptures there is a prophetic element in all human history. For no event stands alone, unrelated, and disconnected. Each is the precursor of something to follow, and contains within itself the germ of future unfoldings. Every generation sows the seed of harvests to be reaped in after ages. This is even more profoundly true when moral principles are involved, and moral and spiritual forces are at work. It is in this view that the historic life of the nations about Israel is brought into the account of the divine administration, and the lesson of God's dealings with them bound up with the record of his oversight and management of the affairs of his own people. In measure, too, it may be affirmed that through all the darkness, tumult, struggle, and suffering of

the ages there survives and abides the hope of
better things to come. It has not always been so
in human consciousness. There have been moments in the life of the world when men seemed
given over to despair, their "hearts failing them
for fear, and for looking after those things which
are coming on the earth." But even then there
have not been wanting true interpreters of the
signs of the times, men who knew something of
God, and dared in the extremes of human depres-
sion to "look up and lift up their heads" in sure
hope of speedy redemption. It is a poor reading
that fails to find God in history; and wherever
God is there is hope for men.

What is true on a broad scale for all the nations
is intensified and condensed into more full and exact expression in the life of the people whom Jehovah set apart for himself. From the beginning
immediately and continuously under divine control, it was shaped and prepared for larger and
better issues. The introductory patriarchal period had in its life the promise and prophecy of
"the good things to come," and in its conscious
communication with God and revelations of his
power and care whenever needed held a pledge
and guarantee of the fulfillment.

It would exceed proper limits to give in detail

the proof and illustration of this statement. It
will suffice to refer to two specific revelations
which, more than any other, furnished the ground
of human hope and were expanded and fulfilled in
the history and institutions of succeeding ages, until they culminated in the coming of the Son of
God.

The one is the promise given in connection with
the curse pronounced upon the serpent; the other,
the covenant made with Abraham.

The first promise comes immediately upon the
catastrophe of the fall. It does not stand alone,
nor is it addressed immediately to Adam and Eve.
The burden of the divine communication is the
curse that was to abide upon the tempter, the
curse of a perpetual degradation below the level
of the lowest brute life, and an undying enmity
between himself and the race whom he sought to
dominate—an enmity which should eventuate in
the complete and final overthrow of his power, in
the penalty of sorrow and subjection denounced
against the woman, and of labor, suffering, and
death upon the man. It was the most impressive
and even exhaustive assertion of the right of God
in his creatures, of the righteous relations between
them as the only ground of human character and
hope, and of the immeasurable evil of sin that could

have been made at that stage of man's life. The promise is set in the midst of the denunciation of the tempter, as though to emphasize the completeness and hopelessness of his ruin and the final failure of his craft and power. On the other hand, its terms stand out strongly against the judgment pronounced upon man as giving assurance that the triumph of the serpent over him should not be final; that even though he should return to the ground from which he was taken, he should yet recover his forfeited estate, and by subjection of the wicked one regain his lost dominion over all things. That his fall was not beyond recovery, that deliverance from sin and its effects was still possible, that a long, uncompromising conflict with sin must be sustained under the conditions of want and pain and death, and that victory should at last be achieved through the " seed of the woman " are the great principles which thenceforth gave direction to the thought and effort of men. The creation groaning and travailing in pain together until now, the weak, confused, and blind endeavors of the world to shake off the burden of wretchedness and find peace for the fearful and clamorous conscience, the indestructible thread of hope that runs through all the tangled web of human affairs, the restrictive and educative prescriptions and sanctions of law, and the glowing and ever-widening anticipations of prophecy, all show how profoundly these first principles wrought themselves into the fiber and substance of our human life. The form of the provision was largely lost sight of. The " seed of the woman " was not retained in the thought and hope of the world, though still the readiness of men to follow any leader who gave promise of a better life showed how intimately the world's hope was associated with belief in the possible achievement of an exceptional human character. Sakya Muni, in the way of self-abnegation; Mohammed, in the way of self-assertion; and Confucius, as a leader in social and national ethics, are in evidence. But within the circle of religious life the truth of divine interposition within the sphere and through the agency of human faculties was held fast and typified and illustrated in many great and successful lives, and became an inspiration and a power to the foremost men of the race down to the time of its final realization in the Son of Man.

In the course of the centuries the almost universal disregard of the ethical character of penalty and promise, even after the judgment of the flood, made necessary a new statement in the form of a covenant. Under the terms of this covenant the "seed of the woman" becomes the "seed of Abraham;" the chosen people, to which the line of descent is restricted, is set apart for God; and the provision for their special training and for the discharge of their high function in relation to God and man is set forth. They were to be the priests of the world. The land of their secluded life, their sanctuary of refuge and worship, was staked off, the disciplinary exile and captivity in Egypt foretold, and their increase and growth in spite of oppression and struggle were assured. The bruised heel, the toil, the pain, the death were the witness to the undying enmity between the serpent and this seed of the woman; while the exodus from the land of slavery and the law under which the commonwealth was organized and the worship of the one true God was instituted and perpetuated, the long line of prophets and saints, and the ever-increasing splendor of prophetic vision and announcement intensified the conviction that the victory should at last be won, and the head of the serpent be bruised by the Son of Man.

It is unnecessary to follow the line of disclosure through all the pages of the Hebrew Scriptures. It is rarely lost to sight even in the midst of darkest and most disheartening conditions. When Israel was at the lowest level, torn by distresses,

10

doubts, and apostasies within, and broken and cast down by assaults without, elect men, the "remnant according to the election of grace," still clung to their faith in promise and covenant, and in jubilant tones proclaimed it to Israel, and held it forth as a standard for the nations. When the fullness of time was come, though the nation received him not, Zachariah and Elizabeth, and Mary, Simon and Anna, and John the Forerunner, and Nathanael, the "Israelite in whom was no guile," and still other true and simple souls, cherished the hope of the fathers, and looked for redemption.

Along with the promise and the covenant there were manifestations of God in forms suited to the condition of men, declaring his constant oversight of human affairs and his unchanging purpose to do all that he had said. We need not trouble ourselves with the difficulties suggested to fastidious and sensitive natures by the anthropomorphisms of these early appearances. It would be hard to conceive of any way of approach to man more appropriate to his character and better fitted to convey the truths intended to be taught. It was from the beginning affirmed that man was made after the likeness of God. It was a natural sequent that God should come near to man in the form which presented that likeness in the region of nature and through the agencies of human speech and action reveal the vital relations between them. The abstractions of the intellect and the creations of the imagination will not serve as the basis of ethical life; and in proportion as they give form and substance to the conceptions of God, they remove men from the sense of truth and reality in their relations to him. The theophanies may be imperfect and defective, as must be all finite appearances; but they make the most direct appeal to human consciousness and the most profound impression upon the moral nature. They do, moreover, represent to us in forms which we can appreciate all that we conceive as highest, best, truest, in being and life; they declare self-consciousness and intelligence, righteousness, truth and love in combination with divine authority and oversight of human affairs. They have a special value to us as a prophetic indication of the form in which the last and complete revelation of God should be made. They point to "the *man* that is my fellow, saith the Lord of Hosts," to that Son of Man who, standing in the midst of men with all the marks of our humanity upon him, could say: "He that hath seen me hath seen the Father." I venture to say that no more complete manifestation of God can be made than is given in the person of him in whom " dwelleth all the fullness of the Godhead bodily." In the light of the eternal day we shall have no more perfect vision of the Father than will be given us in the person of the glorified Son of Man when "we shall see him as he is." Certainly the God of Abraham, of Isaac, and of Jacob, who was "not ashamed to be called their God," thought it no dishonor to himself to come into converse with men upon the ground and within the limits of the nature which he had ordained for them.

Under such impulses given and along the lines indicated in the promise, the covenant, and manifestations of God to the fathers, the historical development of the chosen people proceeded. It was not a continuous, uninterrrupted development. The Scriptures vindicate their own truthfulness by the fidelity with which they record the sins and failures of the tribes, and their pronounced tendencies to break away from the restrictions and safeguards which God had put about them, and become like the nations that were around them. But "the gifts and calling of God were without repentance;" and, while he suffered them to walk in their own ways, and left them to the penalties of their transgressions, he never utterly abandoned them, nor withdrew his oversight and direction of their affairs, nor, indeed, did they entirely lose sight of their relation to him. They fretted under his discipline, and revolted against his rule; but they always claimed a special place in his regard, and in their seasons of distress they cried unto the God of their fathers. The whole course of their history is full of illustration of the principles of divine administration, and furnishes type and instance in abundance of the power of righteousness and of the need and possibility of constant communication with God. In times of extremity, when there was danger of the final apostasy of the nation, or of its complete overthrow, so that it should no longer stand as a witness to the world for him and his promise, God always interposed to avert the catastrophe. Notable instances are given in the plagues of Egypt and the judgment of the Red Sea, the giving of the law from Sinai, the destruction of Sisera and his host, and in later times of Sennacherib and his army. These and many others arrested attention and gave assurance that in all the way of their life God was restraining, directing, and controlling, that he might keep the covenant made with the fathers. Not only was the hope of Israel thus kept alive in some measure among them, but there was always preserved a line of faithful men directly asserting God's right and authority over the people. They were the leaders and commanders of the people whose record is given in brief in the Epistle to the Hebrews. These men were the special depositories of God's power, and conservators of his truth. They were not merely men of official standing. They were priests and prophets of the race by a higher power than the law of a carnal commandment. When the priesthood had degenerated and prophets had become ministers to the will of a corrupt monarchy, they preached righteousness, asserted the claims of God, by miracle if need were, and sustained the faith and encouraged the hope of the remnant that had not " bowed the knee to Baal." In all this there is the same marked reserve and economy of divine force and the same respect for the established order of things which has always and everywhere characterized the working of God. These Scriptures hold us constantly and firmly to the hard ground of common life, and show the plans of God wrought out through the regular processes of his providence. They insist upon the divine origin and relations of man, the divine order of the world, the divine direction of human affairs toward a predestined end—they charge all history heavily with the supernatural element; but they bring in no extraneous forces, and disclose exceptional operations of divine power only when exceptional pressure of evil imperatively required counterpoise and readjustment. The same principle is observed that was declared in our Lord's refusal of signs from heaven. Considering the long periods covered and the immense results sought, the use of the miracle, properly so called, is singularly rare. The exceptional men chosen for his purpose and brought into conscious communion with God, and commissioned and endowed for his work, were not lifted out of the current of human life and above the sense of human companionship. They were men of "like passions with ourselves," and subject to the vicissitudes and evil conditions of their time, nor were they lavish or extravagant in their expenditure of divine resources. They interfered with the ordinary course of events only when the necessities of the divine administration compelled them to do so. Beyond this they did not go. By them and by the special revelations of God it was intended to bring the people to a distinct understanding of the sanctity and high purpose of their life, and of their functions in relation to the world.

Question has more than once been raised concerning the standard of righteousness to which human character and conduct were referred before the Mosaic era. Later estimates of character, which have been framed under the influence and effect of formulated law and experience of its operation, as well as the largely improved instruction in its meaning and application, have taken but little account of the paucity of positive commandments, and the indefiniteness of human relations incident thereto in this early period. But few things by which men could be judged stand out clearly defined until he came who is rightly known as the lawgiver. The nature and extent of ethical obligation were indicated clearly by the revelations which God made of himself. His earliest recorded approach to man was a declaration of his proprietorship in all things, and his authority over his intelligent creatures. "Thou mayest" and "thou shalt not" confer a privilege and impose a restraint. In form it was a commandment, the assertion of a supreme personal will exercising a conscious right. It was extended in the gift of dominion, putting man at the head of creation as the representative of his own rightful lord. Absolute subjection to the will of God and explicit obedience to his command were thus taught as the principles of life. In the penalty of disobedience they found their sanction; while the terms of the promise, pointing

to the undying enmity with the serpent, put him
on guard and set him upon active and unceasing
struggle against the powers of evil.   One after
another the great truths essential to man's life and
relations to God were discovered and became
dominant factors in the thought and life of the
world.   The faith of Abel discerned the place and
meaning of sacrifice, and left it as a basis for all
the religions of earth.   To the perturbed mind of
Cain his own sense of wrong was interpreted and
conscience was thus assigned its place as the witness to right or wrong within man and the warning
against the approach and danger of sin.   The faith
of Enoch brought into immediate experience the
immortality of man.   Noah learned of providence
and judgment, and in practical form preached
righteousness as declared in them for a hundred
and twenty years.   Abraham gathered into his
life all the elements of faith, and laid the foundations of the Church of the faithful upon a basis
so broad that Paul could say the gospel was before
preached to him.   By this appeal to original institutions, as in the case of marriage, our Lord
has taught us to look to natural ordainments for the
ground of natural morality, and given a divine
sanction to the affections and relations of this life,
and set the seal of righteous condemnation upon

the rupture and violation of them. We cannot now tell how far men then understood these things. We interpret them by the light of later days, and can hardly understand and sympathize with the conditions of those to whom the distinct statements of law and the formal exposition of its principles were wholly wanting. They must have known that fidelity to revealed and recognized obligation was the guarantee of the presence and counsel of God according to human need. It was in effect the rule of life given by our Lord: "If any man will do his will, he shall know the truth." On the other hand, the disregard of worship and obedience and the free course given to natural passion and impulse obstructed the way of God's approach and led to blindness and ruin. These things agree with our understanding and experience of character. But to men of that time the application of these principles was not always clear, and had to be learned according to God's method: by processes of discipline. It is not surprising, therefore, that there were found along with a true faith in God and genuine devotion to him many transactions and lines of conduct quite at variance with our ethical standards. We condemn the lapse from truth in Abraham, and the intrigue and chicanery of which Jacob was guilty. But by what known law could they be judged? They were both seeking the fulfillment of promises made by God, and had no legal statement to define these transgressions, and had not yet learned that man's way of working out God's counsels is sure to be the wrong way.

In all this life, principles rather than positive precepts, revelations in response to man's need and call rather than abrupt interference and violent restraint, method of discipline through experience rather than enforced confinement to definite lines, were set forth as appropriate to human freedom and character. No needless burden was imposed. The "liberty" afterward restored under higher conditions was conceded as in the original charter of human rights. The free exercise of the faculties of man, made in the likeness of God, was permitted. It was part of the "wisdom of God" that the world should exhaust the resources of its own wisdom in the management of its affairs and the search after truth.

The place and function of the law are sufficiently indicated by the foregoing statements. The degeneracy of the race, the increasing tendency to evil, the moral obtuseness and the disregard of judgment executed and threatened, put in peril the gracious purpose of God declared in the prom-

ise and confirmed in the covenants with Abraham.
More emphatic statement and more stringent
measures for restraint and instruction were demanded. "The law was added because of transgressions." The enslavement in Egypt and the
deliverance with "the mighty hand, and the
stretched out arm" were the divine discipline preparatory to the giving of the law. The whole period, from the time of the conspiracy of the sons of
Jacob against Joseph, to the exodus, is illustrated
in a brief record of incidents whose significance is
tersely and clearly stated in Stephen's speech to
the Jewish council.

The awe and splendor of the descent of Jehovah upon Sinai gave the law its high sanctions and
set Moses in his seat as its expounder and execu-
tive. It was offered in this form that it might be
known, not only as the rule of individual life and
the basis of social and national polity, but, first of
all, as the ground and condition of their relations
to God. It got its value from its opening statement, "I am the Lord your God, which have
brought you out of the land of Egypt," and referred its ethical quality and its supreme authority
to this assertion of the exclusive right and power
of Jehovah over them. There was not then, as
there never had been, the conception of moral

character apart from divine relations; and it may as well be here noted that moral principles and moral life would never have been possible without some knowledge of God.

The law so formulated was expanded and applied on the religious side as a sacrificial and ceremonial system and on the secular side as a civil polity. In its entirety it is a theocracy, demanding the reference of the entire life of the people immediately to the will and commandment of God.

Its central feature was the priesthood. Under it the people received the law; rather were organized or constituted as a people according to law. The priestly element pervaded and dominated the whole economy. It finds place in the separation of the nation from the common, secular purposes and conditions of other peoples, and the assignment to them of special character and functions in relation to God and the world. They were declared to be a "kingdom of priests and a holy nation." It is expressed with more emphasis in the establishment of a priestly caste, which should be to the nation what the nation was intended to be to the world. Instead of the firstborn from all the tribes of Israel, the tribe of Levi was set apart for priestly function and the service of the sanctuary. It was carried to a higher consecration in

the persons of Aaron and his sons, a family set apai
to minister at the altars, draw near to God, and
declare the mind of God to the people. Of this
family one was set apart as high priest, with exceptional prerogative and exclusive right of entrance into the holiest place of all, the seat of the
Shekinah, the visible representative of Jehovah.
The conception of holiness as essential to the relation to God was carried in all its degrees through
the priestly nation, tribe, and family, until it culminated in the person of the high priest. With
each remove from the wider life without the exac-
tion as to person, character, and conduct became
more minute and thorough, so that finally the
ideal of possible perfection was reached in the
high priest, who alone could come into the immediate presence of God. By thus continually nar-
rowing the circle and enhancing the requirement
as they were brought nearer to God, the conception of the holiness of God was intensified and
exalted.

The sacrificial system is inseparably united with
the priesthood. The priest was ordained to offer
gifts and sacrifices for sin. The offering, whatever its distinctive character, was in recognition of
the absolute right of God in the man, and of the
sin, the weakness, the failure of the man, and

represented confession, self-dedication, and atonement, besides the eucharistic meat offering and peace offering. By expiation, self-dedication, and worship, the sin that separated man from God was put away and renounced and the way of approach to God was opened. The priestly character was thus declared and secured.

The ceremonial system included the declaration and use of places and things and times as holy—devoted to God. Of all these time would fail to tell. The worth and meaning of them are more than suggested in the Epistle to the Hebrews, which, as an exposition of the principles of the old economy, and the link of connection between that and the new, stands unrivaled and alone. Their purpose, together with the limitations of them, is intimated by St. Paul in his references to them when discussing the great features of the gospel, and especially in the Epistle to the Galatians and the cautionary passages of the Epistle to the Colossians. The tabernacle—later in Jewish history the temple—the ark of the covenant, and the Passover were the highest formal expressions of sanctity, and reflected their sacredness and dignity upon the people to whom they pertained.

The civil polity represented the application of these elements to the common life of the nation " as

they were able to bear it." The abominations of
the Gentiles were carefully excluded. Every possible provision was made for the direction of individual conduct and for household order and the
training of the young. The relations between persons, families, and tribes were established upon the
basis of purity and mutual helpfulness. Offenses
that threatened the supreme authority of Jehovah,
or violated the relations essential to the integrity
of the commonwealth as established upon the basis
of divine order were punished with death. Others
suffered graded penalties, for the most part according to the law of relation (*lex talionis*). Where
pardon was possible sacrifices were required and
the priests gave absolution. The minuteness of
detail in every department expressed the jealous
care with which God guarded the integrity of
personal, family, social, and national life on the
secular side, so as to bring it into perfect adjust-
ment and conformity to the high ideal expressed
in priestly life and service.

The breadth and reach of this law have been
discerned by a few of the better minds of later
times. They have seen that the great lawgiver
"builded better than he knew" and established
principles and framed institutions which should
furnish the basis and suggest the methods of all

right government and sound relations, national and international, for the ages to come. As our civilization advances and the conditions of life are better adjusted we come nearer to the old Mosaic economy, enter into truer sympathy with its aims and plans, and gain a higher appreciation of the divine order there declared in the terms and materials of our natural life.

The limitations and inadequacy of all this arrangement are apparent. The promise, the covenant, and the manifold manifestations of God lay back of it and constituted its motive. They were not canceled or forgotten; but the degeneracy of the race compelled more precise and definite expression of them within narrow limits. It was an attempt to declare in outward symbolic form the things that no human speech could utter and no earthly semblance could set forth. Moses was called away from all earthly associations and shut up in the solitude of the mountain alone with God. The things in the heavens were there showed to him—the great divine order of administration stretching through all the years of the future and culminating in " the city that hath the foundations," the vision of whose glory had afore been vouchsafed to Abraham. We can hardly question that, in those forty days when he talked face to

11

face with God, he was granted, in order to the fulfillment of his high commission, a deep insight into
and a true understanding of the great revelations
made before to his fathers. When the long converse with God was ended and his instruction completed, he was sent down to reproduce in visible
form and with earthly material the things that he
had seen. "See," said He, "that thou make all
things according to the pattern showed to thee in
the mount." A grander design than was ever
traced in the mind of the great architect of the
Roman cathedral (St. Peter's) was drawn with
the splendor of the eternal light before him; the
wealth and genius of all Israel were laid under
contribution, and the result was a tent of badgers'
skins in the wilderness. It was a fit type and suggestion of the insufficiency of the legal economy
to declare the whole counsel of God, to show his
righteousness, love, and truth to men—to all men.
"The law made nothing perfect."

Notwithstanding this, there were men who
transcended the limits imposed by legal prescrip-
tion, and caught glimpses of the higher truth suggested by these parables. Like Moses himself,
they were not content with the wonders of Sinai,
the pillar of cloud and fire, Israel's visible guide,
and the cloud of glory that covered the tabernacle;

but with diviner insight and deeper longing urged their importunate prayer: "I beseech thee, show me thy glory." In no mean sense they were products of the law, for without the law they had been impossible, and gave sure token of what the law as a revelation, with its restrictive, educative, and suggestive qualities, could do though it was weak through the flesh. Disparage and depreciate it as we may, the system that could produce men of such mold and stature as those whose measurements are given us in Hebrew song and psalm, in proverb and prophetic teaching, and in achievments whose results have outlasted the centuries and have become incorporate in the best life of the modern world is not to be lightly esteemed. Such men were the true forerunners of the elect band who were found watching at the advent of the incarnate Son, and in their faithful and glad hearts made a home for him when in the midst of the wild, turbulent, hostile elements of the world he had not where to lay his head.

Men of this sort made possible the introduction and permanent incorporation into the life of the nation of prophecy, the last, highest, and most potent factor in the economy of preparation. It was not an absolutely new feature of divine operation. The prophetic element, as already said, in-

hered in history, in virtue of its divine relations and
of the divine oversight and direction which were
never quite wanting in human affairs.   It appeared
as occasion required in exceptional men who recognized the hand of God in the course of events
and announced his purpose and will.   It gave
their character and meaning to the legal dispensation and the life of the chosen people.   It culminated in the special provision of a personal prophetic power and function announced by the
lawgiver himself.   " The Lord thy God will raise
up unto thee a Prophet from the midst of thee, of
thy brethren, like unto me: unto him ye shall
hearken.   According to all that thou desiredst of
the Lord thy God in Horeb in the day of the assembly, saying, Let me not hear again the voice
of the Lord my God, neither let me see this great
fire any more, that I die not.   And the Lord said
unto me, They have well spoken that which they
have spoken.   I will raise them up a Prophet from
among their brethren, like unto thee, and will put
my words in his mouth; and he shall speak unto
them all that I shall command him.   And it shall
come to pass, that whosoever will not hearken unto
my words which he shall speak in my name, I will
require it of him."

Its first intent was to guard against and offset

the unhallowed practices of the nations whom the
Lord cast out before them.   In their eagerness to
search out the unseen and pry into the future they
used divination, enchantments, witchcraft, and
sought unto necromancers and wizards.   To repress this profane curiosity—from which even the
enlightened mind of our own day is not entirely
free, as witness those relics of heathenism known
as clairvoyance, spiritualistic seances, and the
like—and to keep them within the limits of per-
missible and fruitful revelation, God provided for
his people a line of prophets whose word should
be authoritative and final.   It was further intended to relieve them from the awe and terror attendant upon such immediate manifestations of God
as gave sanction to the law at Sinai; and put the
words of God into the mouths of men, that the
channels of our common nature might become the
ways of conveyance for the truth and righteousness and power of God.   Prophecy thus comes
out of its elementary provisional and fragmentary
period and assumes the highest functions known
in the theocratic state.   It interprets promise, covenant, and law, lays its command upon priest, king,
and people, denounces judgment and even gives
assurance of pardon where law refuses remission
and demands death.   Its terms are not limited by

the prescriptions of the Mosaic institute, and its vision is not confined to the needs and fortunes of the Jewish nation. It stands with Isaiah at the threshold of the temple and, though throngs of priests minister at the altars and the smoke of incense pervades the sacred spaces and the chant of the choir resounds in the air, it sees naught but the Lord sitting upon his lofty throne and his train filling the temple, and hears nothing but the music of the seraph's song and the voice of the Lord saying: " Who will go for us?" It was set over the nations and over the kingdoms to pluck up and to pull down and to destroy and to build and to plant. It gathered up the divergent lines of human history and blended them in one in the issues of the distant future. It discharged its final function and completed its work when it turned back to the terms of its own institution and proclaimed their fulfillment in the person of the Lord's Anointed, Son of Man, Prophet, Priest, and King of the race. Upon the manifold phases of his character and person, and the purpose and effect of his work, it lavished the wealth of its imagery and exhausted the resources of thought. In divers degrees and in their varied forms of action and speech all the prophets contributed to the one supreme end; and, drawing in the scattered elements of promise and history, covenant and law, united them in the " man of sorrows . . . bruised for our iniquities," who was yet the " Wonderful, Counselor, the mighty God, the Prince of peace." When that final word had been spoken and the vision perfected, the voice of prophecy was hushed and heard no more until the very presence among men of him " of whom Moses in the law and the prophets did write " once more awoke the slumbering sense of the world, and the forerunner could say: " He stand·· eth among you."

I have here only amplified the brief record of the use made by Peter and Stephen of the prophetic promise and provision. It was the promise of full divine utterance through a human personality to find its last and complete fulfillment in the Son of Man, " in whom dwelleth all the fullness of the Godhead bodily." The holy men of old spake as they were moved by the Holy Ghost, and even so their speech was not final and perfect. It was anticipatory, prophetic, consciously directed to coming generations. It became broader and deeper from age to age, like the waters of Ezekiel's vision that issued out from under the threshold

of the temple and gave the life of hope to the nations. God who spake by the prophets hath at the
last spoken by the Son. The final, perfect, authoritative word is heard. It confirms and is confirmed by all that went before. "And it shall
come to pass that every soul, which will not hear
that Prophet, shall be destroyed from among the
people."

Avoiding all the questions that may be raised by
skeptical inquiry—and which, besides being ir-
relevant to the purpose of this discussion, would
require more elaborate treatment than my time will
allow—we have followed the course of revelation
from its beginning, indicating its character and
noting its contents, that we may find its bearing
upon and relation to the final manifestation of God
in Jesus Christ. If our reading has been true, the
entire record points in one direction. Its germ of
life comes to flower and fruit in him " who is our
life." Its incompleteness is supplemented by the
all-inclusive word of him who spake as never man
spake. In their due order of succession, the
promise, the covenant, the law and the prophets
did their work, each carrying forward the line
handed down to it by its predecessors until the
great representatives of the entire line, Moses and

Elias, surrendered their prerogatives to him whose decease, "which he should accomplish at Jerusalem,"should bring to an end vision and prophecy, fulfill all promise, and vindicate the word heard from heaven: "This is my beloved Son; hear him."

LECTURE V.

THE TESTIMONY OF THE SPIRIT.

(171)

V.

THE TESTIMONY OF THE SPIRIT.

"But when the Comforter is come, whom I will send unto you from the Father, even the Spirit of truth, which proceedeth from the Father, he shall testify of me." John xv. 26.

THE world was about to enter upon the last stage of the long conflict between the serpent and the seed of the woman. The enmity became more pronounced as the words and works of the Son of Man gave more full and complete illustration of the righteous and gracious purpose of God, and evinced itself in an intenser hate and a more malignant persecution. The issue was soon to be joined at the cross; and the event to be determined in other regions, where through death he should destroy him that had the power of death, and declared to the world by the resurrection from the dead. Nor was the world's hate even then to be satisfied. It was to stand in the same attitude of antagonism to his disciples and let fly against them the same fiery darts of persecution. To them, in the absence of their Master, the fortunes of the struggle would seem doubtful, if not hopeless. The majesty of his presence **and his** absolute

(173)

command of all the resources of earth and heaven had sustained and assured them, and they had learned to depend entirely upon him. Against the combined forces of earth and hell the powers committed to them would without him seem to be altogether inadequate. He gives them no promise of relief or respite from the strife. The world would—for his name's sake, because it knew not him that sent him—do to them as it had done to him. Over against this sin and hate and persecution of the world he set the testimony of the Comforter—the Paraclete—which should be their strength and guarantee of success. It is the final provision for his Church, the exhaustion of his resources in the assertion of his right and the extension of his kingdom.

It is no disparagement or depreciation of the foregoing plan and movement of God that brings us, in the development of our faith, to this promise of our Lord as the strength of the Church and the last hope of men. It is but in recognition of the fact that the proportions of the struggle transcend the possible calculations of men and require for its continuance and for the final success of the Son of Man an abiding energy of divine power quite equal to all that was at his command and unembarrassed by the limitations and hindrances of his

incarnate life. We have seen in the record already
made how insufficient to effect the purpose of God
was all the marvelous wealth of revelation and action that had been lavished upon men. As the result of it we have the terse statement of the evangelist: "He [the Word] was in the world, and the
world was made by him, and the world knew him
not. He came unto his own, and his own received
him not." More than that, the men whom he had
chosen out of the world, to whom he had given
the words that his Father had given him and made
known all things which he had heard from his Father, and had said, "Ye have loved me and have
believed that I came out from God," when the
hour of his trial came, forsook him and fled, and
were scattered every man to his own. His personal presence and teaching and their faith and the
love they had for him were not sufficient to save
them from this shameful lapse. Not yet were they
made perfect.

Nor is it as a desperate resort, failing all else,
that we are driven to this last refuge and hope for
the faith of the world. Rather it was in contemplation from the beginning and incorporated as an
indispensable factor in the plan of God and was
the complement, in the order and experience of
human life, of the incarnation. In the old rec-

ords the Spirit of God was the suggested ground
of the law and life of the world and the declared
source of prophetic inspiration, and takes his place
at the last as the fulfillment of that which was spoken by the prophet Joel: "It shall come to pass
in the last days, saith God, I will pour out of my
spirit upon all flesh." It is in perfect agreement
with all that we know of the thoughts and ways of
God that every element in his life, every personality of his being, should be participant in his work
of building up and redeeming the worlds. "Here
the whole Deity is known."

The place which the Holy Spirit fills in the life
of the Son of Man is briefly but suggestively stated. He was the immediate agent in the incarnation. "The Holy Ghost shall come upon thee,
and the power of the Highest shall overshadow
thee" is the announcement of the angel, upon
which is founded the article of the Church's confession, "Who was conceived by the Holy Ghost,
born of the Virgin Mary." John's testimony at the
baptism was the product of the word of God and
the appearance of the Spirit: "He that sent me
to baptize with water, the same said unto me, Upon
whom thou shalt see the Spirit descending, and remaining on him, the same is he which baptizeth
with the Holy Ghost." According to this witness,

the Spirit not only abides upon Christ to give assurance of his possession of all the fullness of the Godhead, but remains at his disposal to effectuate the baptism of all whom the Son shall send him. In his later ministry our Lord promises that from him that believeth on him rivers of living waters shall flow, which he spoke, the evangelist says, of the Spirit which they that believe on him should receive, but which was not to be imparted until he himself was glorified. As the time of his ascension drew near he dwelt more at length upon the coming of the Comforter, and explicitly declared his relations to the Father and himself, and assigned him his functions in relation to the world and the Church.

1. The name given him by our Lord is rendered " Comforter " in our version, which may be used very properly in the old English sense of the word before it became synonymous with " consoler."

It has come to be much used in its Anglicized form—Paraclete—which, as not misleading, may be a better designation, but has the disadvantage of not being understood by the general reader. It is once used by John in his first Epistle: " If any man sin, we have an advocate [Paraclete] with the Father, Jesus Christ the righteous." We

12

are justified in giving it the same signification in the Gospel that it bears in the Epistle. It follows that the Spirit, as the Παράκλητος, represents Christ before men as Christ, in virtue of his propitiation, represents men before the Father; that he advocates his claims and asserts his rights: and as Christ speaks of him as his own substitute, "another Comforter," the meaning counselor, instructor, may be added.

2. Christ, the Son, sends him. He is distinctly and exclusively the messenger and representative of the Son, and undertakes nothing apart from him, or outside of the limits of his mediatorial life and work. He is at one with the Son as the Son is with the Father, and as entirely given to do the will of him that sent him as is the Son. "He shall not speak of himself," said Christ; "but whatsoever he shall hear, that shall he speak. . . . He shall glorify me: for he shall receive of mine, and shall show it unto you." The vague conception of a benignant spiritual influence operating upon the hearts of men, as the fitful breezes of summer move upon their oppressed and languid frames, without distinct purpose or method, is thoroughly disposed of by this sharply defined commission to personal service in exclusive relation to the purpose and work of the Son of God.

3. He is sent from the Father; he proceedeth from the Father. He has his being in the unity of the Godhead, with the Son from the Father, the "fountain of Godhead." The Son is the "only begotten of the Father;" the Spirit "proceedeth from the Father." The Son is sent by the Father; the Spirit is sent by the Father and the Son. For here our Lord says, "Whom I shall send from the Father;" while in a former promise he says, "Whom the Father will send in my name." In both places his indissoluble relation with the Son is affirmed, while his original unity of being with the Father is proclaimed.

4. He is the Spirit of truth. The title indicates that truth is not a matter of formal statement and outward relations to be expressed in creeds and symbols and confessions of faith. It lies deeper. It has vital quality and takes its beginning in the relations of the Godhead. It is here, as elsewhere in our Lord's sayings, "the truth." "The Spirit of the truth" is the reading. "To this end was I born, and for this cause came I into the world, that I should bear witness unto the truth. Every one that is of the truth heareth my voice." In this, his only vindication of himself before Pilate, Christ lifts the truth out of the sphere of this world's life and declares the incompetency of the

natural understanding to originate or apprehend it. He does not attempt to convey it through mere words. He speaks the truth and nothing but the truth; but "the words that I speak unto you, they are spirit and they are life." "The flesh profiteth nothing." "It is the Spirit that quickeneth." His final expression of the truth is himself: "I am the way, the truth, and the life." The truth as it is in the eternal relations of the Godhead, and as it is expressed in the person of the Son, is committed to the Spirit, who will "guide you into all the truth." He is the perpetual guarantee to the Church of God of the possession and final understanding and realization of all the truth.

5. "He shall testify of me." From the day of his ascension the voice of the Son of Man was heard no more among men. On the way to Damascus and in the temple at Jerusalem Paul saw him and heard his voice; and in Patmos John had the vision of his glorified form as he walked in the midst of the seven golden candlesticks, and received from him the messages to the seven churches. But these belonged to the realm of spiritual things. The men who journeyed with Saul saw indeed the light, but heard no articulate utterance; Paul was in a trance in the temple;

and John was in the Spirit. Only through the
Spirit's agency were such conditions and revelations possible. Henceforth the Son was to be
known only through the Spirit.

In the terms of the gospel the testimony of the
Spirit is borne to the world and to his disciples.
In both spheres he follows the line of direction
given in the life, teaching, and work of the Son of
Man. As the Son did nothing of himself, but
availed himself of law and prophecy and the
whole body of divine revelation that went before
his coming, so the Spirit made no independent
disclosures, but brought into clearer light and effective operation the word and life of the Son.
In like manner, as the Son commenced his ministry with the few faithful men, John's disciples,
who were prepared to receive him, so the first
sphere of the Spirit's operation was with the body
of believers instructed and trained by the Lord
himself.

It is well to note again, in this last period of divine movement upon the world, how jealously
God abstains from irregular and abnormal methods of dealing with men. We have seen how
from the first he held himself in reserve, and while
ready to bring forth the illimitable resources of
his divine nature, if the necessities of the case de-

manded them, yet adjusted his work to the conditions and needs of men, and found within the limits of our human life the means best fitted to
achieve his ends. Agencies for working out his
purpose were multiplied and enhanced in efficiency with the growth of the world in experience and
its advance in knowledge and thought. The
powers of mind and life approached more nearly
to the supernatural, and the need for the introduction of forces beyond the possible measurements
of men and for special interferences of God became less frequent and less urgent. We can take
the lesson from our own later history. Ten centuries ago it would have required a series of stupendous miracles to bring about results that enter
into the common experience of our daily life. It
is not with the purpose of depreciating the supernatural or driving it farther away from the thought
and consciences of men that these suggestions are
made. Just the contrary is true. For my part,
holding, as I do, that nature itself is divinely constituted and cannot but be closely akin to and pervaded by the supernatural element, and that every
forward movement in human history and experience has its origin and impulse in the purpose and
power of God, I cannot but be convinced that our
life of to-day is more thoroughly pervaded by su-

pernatural forces than was ever any age of miracle. The eye may not see and the ear may not hear it; but the truest and most real things do not make their voices to be heard in the streets, and are not blazoned in lines of fire across the sky. I do not believe in "natural law in the spiritual world," but I have an invincible faith in spiritual law in the natural world. In taking account, therefore, of the Spirit's work, while recognizing the added resources furnished in the incarnation and the enlarged power of human life, we need not go beyond the ordered methods of divine action known in all previous history.

In pursuance of the same line the operation of the Spirit was, first, upon and within the body of believers. To these men the promise was given. It was a special gift and endowment for their personal guidance and strengthening, and to fit them for the performance of their functions as, in their turn, witnesses to Christ. They were designated and prepared for the reception of the Spirit by the significant action of the risen Lord in the exercise of his newly acquired power: "He breathed on them, and saith unto them, Receive ye the Holy Ghost." It was the breath of the resurrection life. It was a guarantee of the fulfillment of the promise. The Spirit could and would come into the atmosphere of this new life and abide with them forever. "He dwelleth with you, and shall be in you." The Holy Spirit accordingly began his special ministry by coming into direct personal communion with the chosen believers and appropriating and setting them apart for their Lord's service. On the day of Pentecost "they were all with one accord in one place. And suddenly there came a sound from heaven as of a rushing mighty wind, and it filled all the house where they were sitting. And there appeared unto them cloven tongues like as of fire, and it sat upon each of them. And they were all filled with the Holy Ghost." The immediate effect was a distinct and infallible recognition of the Spirit. The appearances as of fire would recall the words of John the Baptist, "He shall baptize you with the Holy Ghost and with fire." But the cloven tongues only sat upon them while they were filled with the Spirit. They made no reference to these, but rather turned at once to the "more sure word of prophecy," "This is that which was spoken by the prophet Joel," and declared its fulfillment with the emphasis of absolute conviction. The misunderstanding, hesitancy, and uncertainty which had so often appeared during their intercourse with their incarnate Lord were put away forever. The perplexity, bewilderment, skepticism, and hostility of the multitude who came together at the hearing of the sound had no effect upon them. The conscious indwelling of the Holy Spirit, making himself known within them, was their introduction. to the realm of spiritual life where doubt and distrust have no place.

It cannot be questioned that our Lord intended to give the strongest possible assurance of the reality of his person and the validity of his claims. The care and thoroughness with which he accumulated the testimonies to himself; the fullness with which he instructed his disciples in them; and his deep, divine yearning for the salvation of men would be but futile and hopeless labor and sorrow unless he could leave in the world a permanent, infallible witness, of equal authority with himself, authenticated by himself and, like himself, self-attesting, and at the same time, witnessed to by the law and the prophets. He had ample experience, among even the best men, of their dullness and slowness of heart to believe. Rabbinism gave him suggestion of the extremes to which higher criticism might go in its handling of the sacred records. The degeneracy and failure of the Mosaic economy gave sure sign of the incompetency of any mere human institution, even though it had a divine origin, to perpetuate the facts and power of his life and work unimpaired and uncorrupted. Nor could he hope that any ecclesiastical succession, however thoroughly furnished at the outset and however maintained, would, by order, symbol, ritual, and ceremony, preserve the truth and conserve the results of his labor, passion, and death. His indifference to all these during his life on earth prove clearly enough that he never intended to commit the fortunes of his Church and the issues of his mediation to any such keeping. If he had so willed it, the order, succession, and ceremonial of Judaism, freed from its animal sacrifices, would have served his purpose better than its late and feeble imitations. It had an unquestioned divine origin, a line of priestly succession reaching far back into the ages of history, traditions of unrivaled splendor, and was the rightful and divinely appointed custodian of the "oracles of God." But himself pronounced the sentence of destruction upon the temple and the polity, and without one written instruction for the faith or order of his Church, sent forth a few unlettered men to preach his gospel, with sure confidence and unerring prevision that through their word and work he should in the end "see the travail of his soul, and shall be satisfied." For he left with them a truer witness and a mightier power than temple and priesthood, law and prophecy, even the Spirit of truth, which should abide with them forever.

The witness becomes the more impressive from the fact that it was an appeal to the individual consciousness, not to the body corporate. They did not acquire the certainty of their conviction from the sound which all heard, nor from the sight of the cloven tongues. Of these last it is said, "It sat upon each of them," as though to emphasize the separate interest and endowment imparted. The more direct and sufficient ground of their certainty was that "they were all filled with the Holy Ghost." The body corporate was to be composed of men, to each of whom the Spirit gave the indubitable witness. In the nature of the case it must be so. Whatever may be the value and power of a general directing influence and overruling hand, such as the providence of God, it cannot satisfy the demand of the heart for immediate communion with God, or supply the need of elevated, devoted lives, evincing their sense of divine companionship, and using the powers of the world to come for the work of this world.

It is part of the record here that they were all filled with the Holy Ghost and began to speak with other tongues as the Spirit gave them utterance. No representative of the body assumed exclusive right and function. Each gave proof of his personal possession of the Spirit and declared his consequent power by personal participation in the work. The same was observed when the gospel was preached to Cornelius, and was so distinctly recognized in the life of the Church that Paul did not hesitate to put the question to some of John's disciples as the test of their relations to the Son of God, " Have ye received the Holy Ghost since ye believed?" Nor according to the faith and practice of that time could any ceremonial act, or form of confession, or ecclesiastical association, or excellence of ethical character supply the place of the conscious possession of the Holy Spirit.

The Spirit, further, in a still higher sense than the Master had done, but following his order of movement, " opened their understanding." The great Teacher brought the resources of his wonderful person to bear upon his disciples, spoke as never man spoke, and added the power of his works to the instruction he gave them. But by the conditions of the incarnation he was compelled to use the languages of earth and speak through organs of flesh. It is impossible from the level of our time to estimate the full effect of his training.

On the one side we note their failures and give heed to his words of reproof, and are disposed to undervalue the elevation and enlargement of mind and character resulting from their association with him. On the other hand, however, we must not forget that they acquired a knowledge of truth in spiritual things and an insight into his character that were shared by no other men of their time, and that after his final teaching during the days of his resurrection life, they only of all men were fitted to be the recipients and depositories of his Spirit. His work was taken up by the Spirit at this advanced stage and carried forward to completion. The Holy Ghost came to them from the divine side, and addressed himself immediately to the spirit of man in them. His entrance was as the touch of the Son of Man to blind eyes, or his voice to the dead. It was the awakening and release of slumbering and imprisoned faculties. The power of spiritual discernment was conferred that they might know the things that were given them of God. They not only, like the prophets, saw a new and higher meaning in life and all things about them, but they perceived the divine elements and spiritual forces expressed and intimated in all the complex and mysterious life of the Son of Man with which they had been so long and intimately

associated.   The things which none of the princes
of this world knew, which eye had not seen, nor
ear heard, and which had not entered into the
heart of man, were revealed unto them by the
Spirit.   For the Spirit did only what Christ had
promised.   He made no new disclosures.   He
brought nothing down out of the heavens that had
not come before.   He took the things of Christ
and showed them to them, and brought all things
to their remembrance whatsoever he had said to
them.   In the Spirit—if I may use in this connection John's suggestive phrase—he showed them
all the scenes and transactions of that memorable
career, as they were looked upon from the height
of the throne.   They could recognize the Lord of
angelic worship in the midst of the lowly surroundings of the stable at Bethlehem; the victor
for our race in the worn and wasted combatant
with the devil in the wilderness; the righful heir of
all this goodly inheritance in the footsore and
weary wanderer by Jacob's well; the titled owner
of all things in the Son of Man who had not where
to lay his head.   Moses and Elias on Hermon's
height were but girded servants waiting at the
gates of the opened heavens to give greeting to the
coming Son, while the voice of the Father from
the cloud of his glory saluted and honored him in

his native right.   The cross was but the gateway
to the grave—the arena of his final victory over
him that had the power of death.   The resurrection life was the outer court to the eternal temple
where he had both worlds in his grasp, one hand
holding the scepter of his priestly rule over all
things, while reaching forth the other that the loving though doubting disciple might put his finger
in the print of the nail.   Though they had known
Christ after the flesh, yet now henceforth they
could know him so no more.   The Spirit had
shown him to them.   So, too, he brought to their
minds all things that he had said unto them in familiar conversation and public speech, parable,
sermon, and prophecy, the interpretations of nature and the expositions of scripture, and gave
them to see meanings that had never appeared to
their natural understandings.   The words were
lost in the realities, the letter in the spirit.   The
variations in gospel narrative and record are not
to be wondered at.   The *things* he said, not the
words he uttered, were brought to remembrance,
and each man, from his own point of view in the
spiritual realm, reproduced them with absolute
fidelity to " the truth " and with small concern for
the earthen vessel of human speech in which it
was conveyed.   Yet they were words taught by

the Holy Ghost, and could not but be true to the divine, deeper meaning of the Lord's teaching.

For, here, it is well to consider that the first outward effect of the gift of the Spirit was upon their speech. They at once began to speak, and as the Spirit gave them utterance. Not only was their stock of language multiplied, but words appeared in new relations and assumed higher significance. They were no longer mere articulate sounds, but living forces. From that time their speech and preaching were not with persuasive words of man's wisdom, but in demonstration of the Spirit and of power. The dull and difficult vocables of earth were transformed into distinct, startling, quickening, and convincing voices from heaven. They preached the gospel—as it ought always to be preached—with the Holy Ghost sent down from heaven.

To this certainty of conviction, opened understanding, and transfigured speech was added the gift of power. In part it may be attributed to the sense of personal elevation and transformation involved in such effects. By the marvelous baptism they had been transferred to a sphere of life where they were consciously beyond the power of mere earthly conditions, and at the command and under the dominion of their Lord only. They possessed and wielded forces unknown to the princes of this world—the powers of the world to come. The feeblest and most timid would be emboldened by such consciousness, to dare enterprises and face difficulties before which the bravest, broadest, and most far-seeing minds of earth would stagger and shrink away discomfited and defeated.

But more than this was intended. Christ had promised the gift of power as a special endowment after that the Holy Ghost had come upon them. It was an attribute of the divine nature which was imparted to them, strengthening their souls and encouraging them in the seasons of peril and suffering; it was, also, that offset to and provision against the destructive power of the world's sin, hate, and persecution which should effectuate their efforts and insure success. It was this consciousness of power not their own, which set them, with the confidence of preordained success and with never a note of hesitancy or uncertainty in their utterance, upon what to the timid and halting Church of to-day seems a desperate undertaking, the establishment of their Lord's rule in all the earth. Nothing was too vast, or too great. "I can do all things through Christ which strengtheneth me."

13

These were the first and decisive operations of the Spirit in fulfillment of the promise of the Son of God. They furnished the Church with the essentials for its work in the world, with the safeguards necessary for the maintenance of its integrity, and with the guarantee for its final success. They had a further significance. They were the formal assertion and assumption by the Holy Ghost of his right as the sole accredited and authorized representative of Jesus Christ in the Church and administrator of its affairs. He set the seal of proprietorship upon every believer. He took control of thought, conscience, heart. They were *filled* with him. In apostolic days the formula of Christian decree was: " It seemed good to the Holy Ghost and to us." To know the mind of the Spirit was the aim of every believer. Even Paul would not have dominion over any man's faith, but was a helper to his joy, and would not have faith stand in the wisdom of men, but in the power of God. The Holy Ghost gave command to the Church at Antioch to send forth Barnabas and Saul. The sin of Ananias was the lie against the Holy Ghost. In all things his supremacy was acknowledged, and no rule was valid without his sanction, and no life was Christ's until he had taken possession of it. "Now if any man have not the Spirit of Christ, he is none of his."

It has still another value as giving illustration and type of the life and methods of the Church and fixing its character in all coming time. It was the simplest conceivable provision. A few men and women assembled in an upper room met the requirement of their Lord, "Where two or three are gathered together in my name, there am I in the midst of them." It was in striking contrast with the elaborate and impressive ceremonial even at that same hour, perhaps, exhibited at the temple. Here were no cathedral splendors, no robed priest, nor smoking censers. nor choral chants. The accidents and incidents of worship were excluded. Yet here was the only authoritative assembly of God's saints on earth; and in the midst of them alone was the recognized and all-powerful representative of the Son of God, the spirit of truth and power. It was his presence that made it the most potent gathering on earth, whose worth should be known and its influence felt ages after the most stately council and the most gorgeous service of the day should have been forgotten. Whatever may be added on the sensuous side, these divine elements and factors can never be dispensed with. The most lavish displays of art, the most seductive appeals to the sensuous nature, the most convincing logic can never fill the place vacated by the Spirit of power. The wealth of nations may be poured into the coffers of the sanctuary, and the resources of genius put at its command; and if brought with true faith and devotion, in genuine acknowledgment of his right to our best and our all, cannot be lightly esteemed. But they that worship him must worship him in spirit and in truth, and the Father *seeketh* such to worship him. That assembly is most highly honored where believing, loving souls have freed themselves most effectually from the distractions of sense, and made the way open to their innermost consciousness for the coming of the Holy Ghost. For all the coming ages this was to be the single and sufficient test of Christian character and standing, in the individual and in the Church.

There is abundant instance given in apostolic writing, in the manifold forms of his working. He is the perpetual and only sufficient witness to the Lordship of Jesus Christ. "No man can say that Jesus Christ is Lord but by the Holy Ghost." He is the one witness to the sonship of the believer mediated by Jesus Christ. "Because ye are sons, God hath sent forth the Spirit of his Son

into your hearts, crying, Abba, Father." To
them that are in Christ Jesus, Paul declares:
" Ye have received the Spirit of adoption, where-
by we cry, Abba, Father. The Spirit itself beareth witness with our spirit, that we are the children of God." " The first fruits of the Spirit"
is the pledge and guarantee of the harvest of our
redemption, " the earnest of our inheritance until
the redemption of the purchased possession."
" The lively hope," the glow and splendor of our
assured expectation of the glory to be revealed to
us, are the effect of the presence and work of the
Spirit within us. He reveals the things freely giv-
en to us of God, takes the things of Christ and
shows them to us, sheds the love of God abroad
in our hearts, makes us to know " the hope of his
calling, the riches of the glory of his inheritance
in the saints, and the exceeding greatness of his
power to usward who believe." He is the fruitful source of all the virtues of Christian character.
" The fruit of the Spirit is love, joy, peace, long-
suffering, gentleness, goodness, faith, meekness,
temperance." He is to give motive, impulse, and
power to all the activities of Christian life. "If
we live in the Spirit, let us also walk in the Spirit." He confers the special gifts which determine each man's place in the Church of God:

"The manifestation of the Spirit is given to every man to profit withal." The word of wisdom, the word of knowledge, faith, gifts of healing, working of miracles, prophecy, discernment of spirits, divers kinds of tongues, interpretation of tongues, "All these worketh that one and the selfsame Spirit, dividing to every man severally as he will." He is the inspiration and power of the preaching of the gospel, as the Acts of the Apostles records, and Peter clearly intimates when he speaks of "them that have preached the gospel to you with the Holy Ghost sent down from heaven;" and Paul, too, when he says that his own preaching was "in demonstration of the Spirit and of power." In brief, the entire life of the believer and of the Church was appropriated by the Spirit. Inward experience, personal virtues, their expression in deportment and conversation, and all the activities of life in every department, were taken under his direction and received their form and vital force from him. The transfer was complete from the region of human passion, impulse, and affection, of secular motive, aim, and influence, to that of spiritual life and power, to the heavenly places in Christ Jesus. It was a new birth of the Spirit which introduced the man into the kingdom of God. He became a new creation; old things passed away, and all things became new. It is impossible to conceive a more absolute assertion of right and a more complete demonstration of power. This was the Church's final charter of her rights, the new covenant in his blood, sealed and attested by the Spirit of promise. This fixes her place and character for all coming time and guarantees to every disciple the full provision for his experience and life in time and eternity. "He dwelleth with you, and shall be in you." "He shall abide with you forever."

It was a priceless gift. It comprehended within itself all that was expressed in the life of the Son from the moment of the incarnation to the ascension, as that life had included all that went before in promise and covenant, law and prophecy. It lifted believers above the dim and misty atmosphere of human conditions and set them in the perfect light of the eternal world. It enhanced their power immeasurably, and gave assurance of indefinite extension of knowledge of divine things, expansion of thought, and elevation of character. It pointed to the heavenly regions in Christ Jesus, as the only true and ample sphere of human life.

It is no wonder that the man to whom these things had become the realities of daily life should denounce in terms of indignation almost divine—

for the fire of the Spirit was upon him—the Church at Galatia, that had so soon removed from this lofty realm and turned again to "the weak and beggarly elements." "Who hath bewitched you?" "Having begun in the Spirit, are ye now made perfect by the flesh?" To our shame be it said, the succession in the line from the Church of Galatia has not been quite lost. Nor is it any wonder that he should come to an utter exhaustion of thought and language in his effort to express the fullness of the blessing of the gospel, and be compelled to place his emphasis at the last upon the "power that worketh in us," "that is able to do exceeding abundantly above all that we ask or think.

We can be at no loss now to understand the words of our Lord to his disciples, so incomprehensible to them at the time and so fraught with sorrow: "It is expedient for you that I go away: for if I go not away, the Comforter will not come unto you." To come into intimate friendship, as he deigned to call it, with his person was the largest boon that had ever been granted to man. It developed, cultivated, and enriched all the best and purest affections of our nature, quickened and intensified the finest sensibilities, elevated and enlarged the mental faculties, as no other agencies nor associations could do. The joy and strength of their life were in him. Even to touch the hem of his garment was to bring forth virtue from him. More than all that he was or could be to them they found in the Spirit. They were brought nearer to him than they were in the flesh, and what of his unsearchable riches he could not communicate through the channels of incarnate life, the Spirit lavished upon them with exhaustless fullness. In their purified and exalted love, they learned to rejoice that he had gone to the Father.

The Lord gave the Spirit as a witness to the world. The world which hated and persecuted him, and would, for his name's sake, continue to hate and persecute his disciples, was to be confronted with the testimony of the Spirit, the only answer to its malignity and the only power to meet and overcome its antagonism. His work in this sphere also is specific and positive. "He shall testify of me." He shall convince the world of "sin, because they believe not on me." He will bring the faith and conscience of men to this sole text. He takes, as always, his line of direction from the Son of God. "If ye believe not that I am he, ye shall die in your sins." The Holy Spirit will know nothing among men but Jesus Christ. The form of his testimony is given.

" He will reprove the world of sin, and of righteousness, and of judgment: of sin, because they
believe not on me; of righteousness, because I go
to my Father, and ye see me no more; of judgment, because the prince of this world is judged."

The conviction of sin is the continuation of the
work of the Son with more ample material and in
higher light. Christ had commenced his ministry
with the preaching of repentance, following upon
John's baptism. He had used the law by which
was the knowledge of sin to the full extent of its
power, and had given it a depth and intenseness
of meaning which it had never known in the hands
of priest or prophet.

He had gone beyond its possible limits and
raised standards of character far above its loftiest
suggestions. He had thus given a deeper meaning to sin and made it more exceeding sinful. All
these higher elements of character he not only exemplified, but made them so essentially and inseparably his own that no man could acquire them
except from him. His own words were to be the
ground of judgment, and the rejection of himself
the supreme and hopeless sin of men. The Holy
Spirit brings the same test to bear from a higher
point of vantage. He takes the things of Christ
and shows them to men—takes his self-renuncia-

tion, his unimpeachable holiness, his vicarious suffering, and the power of his resurrection, and
brings them with the unanswerable appeal of their
truthfulness and divinity to bear upon the conscience of the world. The rejection of the Lamb
of God that beareth away the sin of the world is,
in this light, the supreme ethical evil, because it
involves the perpetuity and final dominion of sin
in the refusal to accept the only provision possible
for its removal. "How shall we escape, if we
neglect so great salvation?" This reference of
sin to the final divine standard of righteousness
and love in the person of the Son of God is the
exclusive work of the Spirit. Neither will any of
the ethical systems of this world succeed in producing conviction of sin, nor will the Spirit use
their arguments or appeals. The ground of all
the systems is infinitely below the level of divine
truth and righteousness. The conceits of philosophy, the secular relations of men, self-interest,
or, it may be, the averments of science which is
yet very far from having spoken its last word, furnish the principles upon which they are framed.
They have succeeded each other in the cycles of
human thought, and each has lasted only until the
next in order has come and searched it out.
Among them all there has been no reference to a

final and absolute tribunal of right from which no
appeal can be taken, and in whose decisions the
conscience finds final settlement of all its doubts.
But when the Spirit with divine authority sets before the conscience the claims of the incarnate,
crucified, and risen Lord, conviction is absolute.
There may be struggle, resistance, even lapse into
moral indifference and death; but argument and
appeal are felt to be impossible. The question is
settled at once and forever; the consciousness of
sin, dulled and latent it may be, but indestructible, remains with the man, and, when the final
judgment shall be set, indictment, plea, and answer will be needless formalities. "And he was
speechless."

Another sense has been given to the words " because they believe not on me." They are taken
to mean that the Spirit will convince of sin because Christ's life and words had failed to produce
the effect. In this view they merely emphasize
the need of the Spirit to work conviction without
special reference of the sin to Christ's person. It
is an entirely inadequate view, at variance with
the trend and final effect of our Lord's teaching
concerning himself. His life was a failure only
so far as human observation could go. On the
divine side it was the most triumphant success

ever achieved in the history of men or angels. He was not taken to his Father's house in the silence and sorrow of defeat.

> Cherubic legions guard him home,
> And shout him welcome to the skies,

while the everlasting gates lifted up their heads that the King of glory, the Lord strong and mighty, should come in.

Nor did the Spirit come to men to tell of disaster and failure. He came with assertion of right in behalf of the risen and triumphant Lord. There was need for the Spirit, because he could reveal the Son of God as he could not be known under the forms of fleshly life. He could reach the inner sense of man as it could not be reached through fleshly organs. He was and is under no restrictions of the sensuous nature. He belongs to the realm of eternal realities, and can come without hindrance to the very heart of our humanity.

Over against this conviction of sin in the world, tne Spirit is to bear witness to righteousness, "because," said Christ, "I go to my Father." It has heretofore been urged that righteousness is not formal, conventional, the product of human relations, but that it has its origin in the personal relations in the interior life of the Godhead, is

manifested in the absolute devotion of the Son of
Man to the will of the Father, and has its final
illustration in the sacrifice of the cross, made on
one side to the will of the Father, and on the
other to his love for the world; by which sacrifice he, at the same time, made provision for the
impartation of righteousness to men. He is " the
Lord our righteousness." No other among men
has ever been offered as an authoritative and recognized type and standard of righteousness for all
men and all time. The vision of his glory would
soon have become dim and the lines of his perfect
features marred and finally effaced had the world
been left to its own rivalries and passions and
blind strugglings. Jerusalem had already almost
forgotten him when the sound from heaven called
together the startled multitude and Peter preached
him risen from the dead, exalted to the right-hand
of God, and still holding converse with men by
his Spirit which he had shed forth. The splendor
of his righteousness was reproduced in terms of
the Spirit in the consciousness of men. The failure of the world to retain God in their knowledge
and the want of fixed ethical excellence already
spoken of, as well as the degeneracy of moral
forces in our human nature, and the effect of the
coming of the Son of God in exciting hate and

persecution even unto death, shut us up to the work and witness of the Spirit as the only hope of righteousness for the world. He speaks from the heart of the Father in the name of the Son. He passes by the formal discussions and artificial distinctions of the human intellect, gets beneath the jarring and shifting conventionalisms that order human relations, sweeps aside the shallow pretenses of selfish passion, and brings the heart and conscience of men face to face with the eternal order, the divine righteousness embodied and expressed in Jesus Christ. Henceforth there is no possibility of righteousness but in Christ, and " they that hunger and thirst after righteousness " come to him that they may be filled.

His final witness is to judgment. " Of judgment, because the prince of the world is judged." The separation between the sin of men under the dominion of the prince of the world, and the righteousness of the Son of God is declared when he goes to the Father. He goes where he was before. He leaves them where he found them. They are from beneath; he is from above. In the strife between them, though they had done what they listed and had been aided to the extent of his power by the prince of evil, he had maintained his integrity, unswervingly done the will of

his Father, borne the burden of the cross, and the
humiliation of death, and coming forth from the
grave triumphant, "declared to be the Son of
God with power." The cross was the judgment
of this world; the resurrection, the final defeat of
the prince of this world. He could not hold the
soul of the Son of God in death, nor prevent his
return to earth and reassertion of his right over
the race he had won by his sacrifice. Righteousness had its complete and final triumph when he
cried, "It is finished," and went to his Father.
The judgment and condemnation of the prince of
this world is repeated and emphasized by the
Spirit in the deepest convictions of even the men
of this world. Enervated souls in the Church of
Christ may truckle to his arrogance and men of
the world may frame shallow defenses and shield
the enormity of their crime behind the splendors
of wealth and the delights of sense; but the judgment has been pronounced, Satan has fallen from
heaven, the prince of this world is cast out, and
in every open conscience the Spirit of God repeats: "Whosoever will be a friend of the world
is the enemy of God."

In the due course of action the Spirit extends
his witness through the agency of men and by the
ministry of the word. How far and how effect-

ively he carries his work beyond this limit and through other channels we may not know. God has never left himself without witness among the Gentiles; and it is hardly to be thought that in this last, richest, and broadest dispensation of his grace they should be left entirely out of the reckoning. "Uncovenanted mercies" have been spoken of. There are none such. The first promise was for the entire race. The covenant looked to all the families of the earth. The heathen nations were in contemplation of law and prophecy, and the new and everlasting covenant in the blood of Jesus Christ embraces all that was ever proposed, and in its terms is broader than all that preceded it. The Holy Spirit can find means of reaching men that we know not of, and we may be sure will enter every open way that leads to a human conscience. Did the prophecy which Peter declared fulfilled on the day of Pentecost reach no farther than the Jewish multitude? or did the subtle, divine influence extend itself over the wide areas of heathendom and beget a sense of want and unrest, stir within the souls of men a secret, indefinable longing which could not be uttered, and make them look upward for some rift in the closed heavens that had so long concealed the mysteries of God and life and hope? Was the Spirit poured

14

upon all flesh? Most assuredly the world's movement has been upward from that hour. "Earnest
expectation" has been the feature of the world's
life in all the centuries since. It has brought strife
and change, and must continue to do so until men
know him that speaks and consent to follow his
guiding.

We have followed the course of testimonies
through all the developments of human history. If
we have rightly understood them, the dominant and
indispensable element in them is supernatural. It
is divine. It is none the less so because it has
taken on natural forms and made its appeal to us
through the organs and channels of our humanity.
That itself is of God and is God's chosen way of
making himself known. He has adjusted himself
to the changing conditions of human life and has
had his part in the advance movement of all the
ages. When the fullness of time was come the divine purpose and action culminated in the incarnation. Then the heavens were broken wide open,
and all the supernatural forces were drawn to earth
and accumulated in and about the person of the
Son of God. Held in restraint by the conditions
and necessities of his work, they were set free by
his resurrection from the dead; and thenceforth,
under the direction of his Spirit, they became, as

they are, the dominant factors and forces in the life of the world. The hard conditions of life continue. We lie down in the wilderness and have naught but a stone for a pillow; but the heavens are opened over our heads and the angels of God are ascending and descending upon the Son of Man. Here is our Bethel. The Lord is in this place. This is none other than the house of God, and this is the gate of heaven. Here we have the certitude of our conviction. All testimonies converge upon one form. The scars may be in his hands, and the anguish of death in his eye; but we fall before him with the worshiping cry, " My Lord and my God." " Blessed are they that have not seen, and yet have believed."

LECTURE VI.

THE TESTIMONY OF THE CHURCH.

(213)

VI.

THE TESTIMONY OF THE CHURCH.

"Ye shall receive power, after that the Holy Ghost is come upon you: and ye shall be witnesses unto me both in Jerusalem, and in all Judea, and in Samaria, and unto the uttermost part of the earth." Acts i. 8.

THE essential facts of the gospel, the things relating to the person of our Lord Jesus Christ, his "power and coming," have thus far occupied our thoughts. The life of Jesus of Nazareth has been pressed upon our attention with the imperious demand that we recognize and accept it as the veritable and final manifestation, the complete revelation of God to this world. It is not enough that it be conceded that the phenomena of his life were wonderful beyond all the wonders of antecedent prophetic and miraculous life and action. There is a constant assertion of the immediate and eternal relation of the Son of Man to the inner life of the Godhead, that he is in nature and substance the Son of God. There are no possibilities of divine being and action which he does not appropriate to himself; and he makes the validity of his claim the only ground of hope for

(215)

the world, and the rejection of it the sin and ruin of men.

In proof of facts of such breadth and import he could not and did not rely upon anything less than the authority and attestation of the Father himself. He was the only competent witness to these things that lay hidden within the mystery of the Godhead. No man could come to the Son except the Father should draw him. He must be taught of God. The divine nature in the Son manifested in his life and works made direct appeal to the ethical and spiritual nature in man. The divine utterances through the ages before, in divers forms and degrees, as the world could bear them, the "Oracles of God," reënforced the appeal, as they had prepared the way for it, and discharged their contents into this last and only complete expression of God.

When this vast body of divine testimony had been accumulated and perfected in the life, death, resurrection, and ascension of the incarnate Son, it was committed to the Comforter, the Holy Spirit, who alone was sufficient to reveal and interpret it to men.

In all this it has been clear that the testimony must correspond to the facts. In so far as these were within the compass of secular life and pertained to the historical order, witness must be taken from that sphere and tried by its laws. If they were eternal, divine, the "voice from the excellent glory" the habitation of the Most High, must proclaim them. For the things of God knoweth none but the Spirit of God.

The nature of the testimony being determined and the sum of it completed, it remains only to know how to make it available. On the divine side the Spirit, as heretofore seen, is commissioned to take the things of Christ and show them to us, to convince the world. On the human side the line and method of God's procedure remain unchanged and unbroken.

1. "*Ye*," said Christ, "are witnesses." Men "of like passions with ourselves," not even of "the princes of this world," who had shown no very sublime heroism in the emergencies of their life, rather commonplace, though on the whole honest, earnest, well-meaning, even devoted men, whom the Lord had chosen, trained, and commissioned, were charged with this high function and immense responsibility. Whatever was to be done must be done through human agency. Not yet, nor indeed until the end, were the legions from the eternal world to be called into active service. "For unto the angels hath he not put in subjec-

tion this world to come, whereof we speak." In silent, unseen ministries they may wait upon the heirs of salvation. But they cannot enter into the strife. As in the wilderness, they come for such service as they may render when the fight has been fought. The conflict is still with the " seed of the woman; " and to our nature are intrusted the immense, unsearchable resources of the gospel, which is the power of God, to be used through human organs and faculties until the end is reached.

It is our Lord's final assertion of the dignity and worth of our nature. By the incarnation he had raised man above the common life of this world, declared his constant, unobstructed communion with God, and made him recipient of influences and powers belonging to the eternal kingdom. By this final commission and endowment he incorporated men into the divine plan and charged them with the responsibility of carrying forward the plan to its completion, so making them " workers together with God."

2. The value of the human element is determined, as was the divine factor, by its relation to the Son of God. As all divine revelation and action hitherto had converged upon the Son, and through him alone life, light, and power had come

to the world, so now henceforth men were to be
reckoned according to their relations to him.
They were to be baptized into him, must have the
mind that was in him, seek and set their affection
upon things within the realm of his supremacy,
"where Christ sitteth at the right-hand of God."
Christ was to be all in all.   All the motives, impulses, affections, and powers of their life must
come from him and move toward him.   Qualified
by such willing surrender and devotion to him and
by the training, first given by himself, and provided in the teaching of the gospel and the providential discipline of life, they were assigned, each to
the special place and work for which he was fitted,
all to the one work of making known and establishing in the heart and life of the world the
claim of the Son of God as the supreme and only
Ruler and Lord of this and all worlds.

3. Their function as witnesses demanded immediate and personal knowledge of and participation in the truth.   They are not brought into a
school to be instructed in forms, principles, and
systems of doctrine, and thence sent forth to pro-
mulgate theories and enforce them by rational and
educational processes.   They were witnesses to
facts, none the less facts because in the substance
and essentials of them they lay beyond the range

of human observation, eternal facts which could be apprehended only as God is apprehended, as anything and all things outside the region of sensuous perception and mere intellectual conception must be apprehended. The language used by these men in after years shows that they understood the exigencies of their situation and conformed themselves thereto with all fidelity. " We cannot but speak the things which we have seen and heard " was the expression of their sense of obligation and responsibility. These things were not matters of casual observation or discovery, nor had they been brought to their knowledge for their personal benefit alone. They had been communicated to them by the choice and according to the purpose of God, that they might speak them forth to all who would hear. They were " witnesses chosen before of God." The opening verses of the first Epistle of John express with strong emphasis the whole case. " That which was from the beginning, which we have heard, which we have seen with our eyes, which we have looked upon, and our hands have handled, of the Word of life; (for the life was manifested, and we have seen it, and bear witness, and show unto you that eternal life, which was with the Father and was manifested unto us;) that which we have seen and heard declare

we also to you, that ye also may have fellowship
with us: and truly our fellowship is with the Father,
and with his Son Jesus Christ." Both elements,
divine and human, are distinctly recognized and
expressly affirmed. "That which was from the
beginning, "the Word of life," the "eternal life,
which was with the Father"—these realities of
the eternal world are the body and substance of
the communication to be made. "We have heard,"
"we have seen with our eyes," "we have looked
upon, and our hands have handled," "the life was
manifested unto us," "we have seen and heard"—
declared in most positive form the reality and absolute certainty of the knowledge conveyed to them
through their human faculties; while the divine
process is more than intimated in the statement
that "the eternal life which was with the Father
was *manifested* unto us." The reason for the
manifestation stands in the terms "we bear witness and show unto you . . . that ye also
may have fellowship with us." Their personal
experience was to be communicated to others, that
they also might be participant with them in the
eternal life in which they themselves had become
partakers with the Father and with his Son. In
such terms they declare the certainty of the things
wherein they instructed men, became the human

sponsors for the truth of God, held themselves an-
swerable for its maintenance and propagation and
affirmed the right and power of men through their
word to come into the same relations to the Father and the Son and realize in themselves that
eternal life which was with the Father.

They were not unmindful of the fact that in one
principal aspect they stood before the world as did
their Lord. Their claim would be challenged, and
must be vindicated. In a case of such moment the
witnesses must be unimpeachable. Yet their record was not perfect. They could tell of their personal association and intimacy with their incarnate
Lord, give the details of his life and death, with all
the marvelous attendant phenomena, and declare
that they had seen him risen from the dead; but
were compelled to admit that they had very imperfectly understood him while he was with them;
that they had had so little confidence in him that
when he was subjected to the dreadful ordeal of
trial, condemnation, and death by the cross they
had forsaken him, and even after they had seen
him in his resurrection life they had such feeble
conception of its meaning that they remained long
in doubt and indecision. Not until he was gone
from them did they really know him. The human
element had dominated them until the decisive

hour when they received the Holy Spirit. They now propose to intrust their own vindication and the sufficiency of their testimony to the same power which had interpreted the truth to them and established them in the faith.

4. "Ye shall receive power after that the Holy Ghost is come upon you." It was an imparted power, not the natural result of a higher enlightenment, nor the development under new conditions of a natural capability hitherto latent and unsuspected. It was a positive energy exhibited, first, in the confirmation of their faith and the appropriation of every faculty of mind and life for its support and propagation; and then, in giving vitality and force to their utterance of every truth of the gospel. "With great power," it is said, they gave "witness to the resurrection of the Lord Jesus." Their preaching, as Paul's, was in "demonstration of the Spirit and of power." Nothing like this had ever been known in the circles of this world's wisdom and teaching. Men of exceptional faculty and extraordinary endowment have profoundly affected their own age and even extended their influence, directly or indirectly, through succeeding generations; but none of them have been able to command and establish faith in themselves and their words so absolute

that it could withstand all forms of opposition and persecution, and project itself in its integrity and with unabated vigor of life through all the changes of the after centuries. By the introduction of this element of power into their speech and life these witnesses to Christ, men of common mold, were enabled to make direct and effective appeal to all the various modes of thought and life in their own time and send it, a resistless and controlling force, into the new and unforeseen civilizations of later times. The word and the power went together. It was this that differentiated Christian preaching from human teaching.

5. The power was the immediate result of the coming of the Spirit. Its quality is thus distinguished from every form of earthly force. It belongs to the spiritual realm, and is not an attribute or attendant of the sensuous nature. It comes in upon the side of our nature that is in nearest relation to the eternal world, and in its expression is in perfect agreement with the entire course of divine revelation. It is not a subjugating force, but a power imparted. It enables, not overpowers. "Where the Spirit of the Lord is there is liberty." The will has the sphere of its energy widened, and the understanding is brought into clearer light. The specific promises of the incarnate

Lord look to this enhancement of ability, enlargement of knowledge, and sense of freedom, and
guarantee them in the gift of the Spirit.

Upon these terms the Church of God is constituted. It is the congregation, association, community of men, called of God, to whom the Holy
Spirit has shown the things of Christ and imparted
his power that they may be his witnesses in all the
world. This is the fulfillment of the word of
Christ: "Upon this rock will I build my church;
and the gates of hell shall not prevail against it."
The divine revelation of the Son of the living God
to the consciousness of men is the sure foundation
of the Church and its impregnable defense against
the fiercest and most malignant assaults that can
be directed against it.

The divine element is continuously and most
prominently set forth in every apostolic address to
the Church and statement of its character; and
everything that will not comport with this is carefully excluded from the conception and represen-
tation of it. "Chosen in him," "called to be
saints," "in Christ a new creation," and many
such expressions show how far removed, in the
thought of the apostles, was the Church of Christ
from the idea of any mere earthly association or
life, and how thoroughly it was pervaded by su-

15

pernatural forces and its life identified with that
of the eternal world. "Our citizenship is in
heaven" is the confident utterance of a soul in
conscious and glad fellowship with "the general
assembly and Church of the firstborn, which are
written in heaven." Whatever defects may have
appeared in the human, the earthly manifestation,
and however imperfectly it may have been developed, this idea and ideal was always present to
the minds of the apostles and gave form and meaning to all their instructions. They made no appeal
to earthly motives, suffered the intrusion of no
earthly influences, and pointed to no earthly ends.
They offered only a divine model of life and
character: "Be ye followers of God as dear children." "Let this mind be in you which was also
in Christ Jesus." They recognized "the love of
Christ," "the Spirit of Christ," "the powers of
the world to come," "the fellowship of saints"
as the legitimate forces constraining men to all
holy conversation and godliness. They kept
thought and attention fixed upon "the things
which are not seen," "things above, where Christ
sitteth at the right hand of God." They hoped for
the "inheritance incorruptible, undefiled, and that
fadeth not away, reserved in heaven for them who
are kept by the power of God through faith unto

salvation ready to be revealed in the last time,"
"for the new heavens and the new earth wherein
dwelleth righteousness," "for the city which hath
foundations, whose builder and maker is God."
They cherished the longing for the coming of the
Son of God, "the revelation of Jesus Christ," as
the consummation of their hopes and the end of
all their labors. The single condition and vital
element of this super-terrestrial life was the faith
which is "the substance of things hoped for,
the evidence [or conviction] of things not seen."
"The just shall live by faith." We "walk by
faith, not by sight." "This is the victory that
overcometh the world, even our faith."

Without these high, spiritual qualities and faculties no man is competent to bear witness to the
Christ. For he must speak the things which he
has seen and heard. How entirely inadequate
and ineffective for the purposes of the gospel are
the gathered resources of this world's wisdom,
has already been set forth. It is undoubtedly true
that the effect of the incarnation upon the human
side of our life is of inestimable worth. We owe
to that all the finest and purest elements of what
we call our Christian civilization. It has ennobled
manhood, elevated womanhood, refined human
relations, given birth to chivalry, made the broth-

erhood of men the 'watchword of nations, proclaimed liberty to captives, and written hope for
humanity upon every page of history. The
streams of beneficence and charity that have made
glad and fruitful such vast wilderness places of
this world have come, though often by tortuous
channels and with turbid waters, from that fountain. We cannot depreciate these any more than
we can speak lightly of Christ's ministries of
mercy to the sick, the hungry, and the degraded,
though often they went no deeper than the bodily
life. But the refinement and culture and even the
higher ethical life of this world are not the qualifi-
cations in virtue of which men may witness to the
Son of God.

> What we have felt and seen,
> With confidence we tell;
> And publish to the sons of men
> The signs infallible.

The most luxuriant imagination, the most persuasive eloquence, and the utmost vigor of logic
cannot compensate for the lack of the spiritual
faculty and the spiritual knowledge. Now can
the Church as an organized community dispense
with these marks of her divine origin and relationship and assurance of power and success. No
historic order of ministry, no beauty and per-

fection of service, no luster of achievement in the
world of art and letters, and no triumphs in the
fields of civilization and government will suffice to
establish her claim as the witness to the Son of
God. "Thou hast a name that thou livest, and
art dead" has been written of many a successor
to the church at Sardis. Rome is not the authorized symbol of the divine commonwealth. It is
"Jerusalem which is above, which is the mother
of us all."

It is now not difficult to give in outline the form
of the testimony for which the Church of God is
responsible.

1. It is bound to reproduce in individual and
ecclesiastical life as nearly as possible the ideal of
the Lord's life and work.

In personal experience the conformity to the
image of the Son of God is to be attained by the
processes prescribed by him. Repentance, whose
meaning is given in the words of Isaiah, "Let the
wicked forsake his way, and the unrighteous man his
thoughts" changes the attitude of the man toward
the world and divine things, puts them in due relation
and proportions before him, and prepares him for
the revelation of the things of God, the kingdom of
heaven. "Repent, for the kingdom of heaven is
at hand!" was the preaching alike of John and of

Jesus. Faith, the conviction and discernment of invisible and eternal things, apprehends the true, divine character of the Christ, the Son of the living God, begets a sure trust and confidence in him as the Saviour of them that believe, appropriates the entire provision of spiritual blessing in the heavenly places in him, and becomes the pervading element and potent factor in character and life. " By it the elders obtained a good report;" and every great discovery and achievement in the realm of spiritual life has been made by faith. When these conditions are realized the work of the Holy Spirit is effectuated in regeneration. The man is born again and enters into the kingdom of God. He becomes a new creation. Old things are passed away, and all things are become new. His relations are fixed in the divine order; and he becomes a participant in the righteousness, truth, and purity, the affections and the power of the divine life. His sonship through Jesus Christ is declared, and the Spirit bears witness with his spirit that he is a child of God. The fruit of the Spirit—love, joy, peace, long-suffering, gentleness, goodness, faith, meekness, temperance—appears in his character and experience and gives divine fullness to his life and determines his ethical relations to men. Nor is it a single, limited, and final transaction. According to the unvarying law of God's dealing with men, there is constant growth in grace and knowledge. By the processes of ordained discipline and the continuous operation of the indwelling Spirit his faculties are quickened and developed, his insight into divine things becomes more and more clear, broad, and deep, and his consciousness of fellowship with the Father and with his Son Jesus Christ more intense and uninterrupted. He grows up into Christ his living Head in all things. Through the stages of childhood and youth he passes to maturity of spiritual life and becomes a perfect man in Christ Jesus. To what extent the growth may be carried by the gracious leadings of the Holy Spirit it is impossible to say. The resources of truth and power in the gospel are beyond human reckoning. The riches of Christ are unsearchable. The one example and model furnished us is in the person of the Son of Man. The freedom and fullness of his spiritual life, his unobstructed and constant intercourse with the Father, the breadth and depth of his knowledge of eternal things, the ease and completeness with which he appropriated to himself the powers of the invisible world and his perfect joy in all these seem to set him beyond the possible approach of common men. He uses for himself terms of universal import. "The Father loveth the Son, and showeth him all things that himself doeth." "All things that the Father hath are mine." But he withholds nothing of all from those that love him. "I have called you friends; for all things that I have heard of my Father I have made known unto you." "If a man love me, he will keep my words, and my Father will love him, and we will come unto him, and make our abode with him." "These things have I spoken unto you, that my joy might remain in you, and that your joy might be full." With utmost emphasis of speech he strives to fix in him the conviction that there is nothing in the divine life, or in the whole region of heavenly things belonging to himself, in which he will not make them partakers in the measure of their love and obedience.

His words fully justify the apostles in the use of terms that seem to indicate that conscious Christian life knows no limit. In Paul caught up into the third heaven and John in converse with his glorified Lord and gazing through the open door upon the inner life of the excellent glory—exceptional moments, it may be, in Christian history—there are illustrations of attainments not beyond the reach of true and simple faith. Even these can hardly exhaust the import of the prayer of

Paul for the Church: "For this cause I bow my knees unto the Father of Lord Jesus Christ, of whom the whole family in heaven and earth is named, that he would grant you, according to the riches of his glory, to be strengthened with might by his Spirit in the inner man; that Christ may dwell in your hearts by faith; that ye, being rooted and grounded in love, may be able to comprehend with all saints what is the breadth, and length, and depth, and height; and to know the love of Christ which passeth knowledge, that ye may be filled with all the fullness of God. Now unto him that is able to do exceeding abundantly above all that we ask or think, according to the power that worketh in us, unto him be glory in the Church by Christ Jesus throughout all ages, world without end. Amen."

It is not helpful to the breadth, freedom, and power of the gospel to reduce the terms of Scripture—terms of the Spirit—to the limits of technical definitions. There are no measurements by which we can stake off and in a quasi-materialistic way map out the ever-enlarging regions of spiritual life. In the glowing and broadening perspective of the glories that lie before us we give but little heed to the steps of the way, and do not pause to count the milestones of our progress.

Forgetting the things that are behind, we reach eagerly forward toward those that are before. The only rule given is the divine one: "To him that believeth all things are possible."

This personal experience is sustained and advanced by the methods indicated in the Word of God. Foremost among these is the faithful study of the Word itself, not in the critical way that we may become familiar with the letter of it, test its historical value, appreciate its forms, or avail ourselves of its prudential regulations for the direction of our secular life; but with reverent, devotional spirit that we may learn what is the will of God in Christ Jesus concerning us, find out what God is and what his relations to men, what his work is in this world and how he will have us to work together with him. "The letter killeth" cannot be forgotten. We search the Scriptures— if we use them rightly—because in them we think we have eternal life, the life that is in the Son of God, of whom they testify. Their worth and power are known only to those who by constant prayer keep them in close and living relation with the eternal world. For the light that clears their pages must come from God, who declares himself in them; and the power that is conveyed through the oracles of God is the power of the Holy Ghost,

who moved holy men of old to speak and to write
them. Prayer, direct intercourse with God, including worship, thanksgiving, petition, is limited
in its results only by the need, the spiritual capabilities, and the faith of the man, on the one side,
and on the other, by the resources of God. It
gains in intenseness and power by Christian fellowship. Participation in public worship and the
ordinances of the sanctuary broadens and intensi-
fies sympathy and adds a deeper, living interest to
prayer. He who wrote "Forsake not the assem-
bling of yourselves together" understood the law
of the communion of saints. To these more directly spiritual forms of duty and service must be
added the individual witness to Christ in every
station and vocation of life. The boldness of the
apostles is recorded as our example. The silent,
unobtrusive ministries of a Christlike life, the
conduct of business in his name and in obedience
to his word, the chaste conversation which brings
all the associations of life under the hallowing influence of his Spirit, are the common and univer-
sally required testimonies to the name and power
of the Son of God. But the open and uttered acknowledgment of personal relation to him, the
sometimes aggressive assertions of his right, the
confession of him before men are indispensable to

the vigor and success of Christian life. "God hath not given us the spirit of fear," and the cowardice that is ashamed of the testimony of our Lord gives small promise of the speedy fulfillment of the great commission of the Church.

The power of individual life thus quickened, furnished, and kept in immediate relation with the Son of God is beyond all estimate. The want of it can be supplied by no form or force of mere ecclesiastical system. It has, more than once in the course of human history, been the prop and stay of a falling Church and the only guarantee of the perpetuity and success of the Church of God. It is the rock upon which Christ builds. But the completeness of it can be found only in association with all that are like-minded. The communion of saints is necessary to the perfection of the saint. "They without us shall not be made perfect," is the underlying principle of the divine commonwealth. While our Lord had respect to the single soul and made full provision for its life, freedom, and power, he had in contemplation the community of his disciples, the congregation of believers, and put them under such obligations of love not only to himself, but to each other, that they should be constrained into closest intimacy and fellowship of life and come by natural law and process into organic unity. He did not bind them together by the outward forms of organization and institution, by the law of a carnal commandment. They were held by the power of the indissoluble life, in virtue of which they would grow into one—into the unity of the faith and of the knowledge of the Son of God.

2. To this body of faithful men was given the charge to secure and convey to the world the testimony in support of the claims of its Lord. According to the direct promise of Christ it was to be guided into all truth and put in remembrance of all things that he had said to them by the Spirit. His words had included the exposition and interpretation of the Old Testament writings. They were thus made the custodians of the oracles of God, which had been before committed to the Jews. In pursuance of the method used by the holy men of old they put into permanent form the things which they had seen and heard, chronicled the initial and typical movements of the Holy Spirit, and gave instruction in all matters of faith and practice pertaining to the new life. The result remains to us in the gospel narratives, the Acts of the Apostles, the apostolic Epistles, and the Apocalypse of John. The record thus made under the direction of the Holy Spirit gave to the Church of the future

security against the vagueness and uncertainty of tradition passing through the ever-changing conditions of human thought and speech, furnished the final test of every doctrine and practice imposed, by whatever authority of school, Church, or State, upon the conscience of men; set the divinely ordered utterance, with the unfailing accompaniment of the Spirit, the Guide to truth, over against the claims of dim and easily misunderstood intuitional claims, and maintained the authority of the Son of God expressed in his word and spirit against the insinuations and assertions of every form of rationalism. No miracle was wrought in fixing the canon of Scripture or preserving the letter of the text. It would have been distinctly at variance with the recognized way of God to interfere after this sort with the responsible human agency. The faith and love and spiritual discernment of the Church were trusted to decide the questions that were raised upon the place and value of each book. It was only after careful comparison with other scriptures, due test in the experience and life of believers, and faithful scrutiny of its claims to authenticity and genuineness that each of the recognized writings was admitted to the canon. The human element was allowed its largest freedom, but that human ele-

ment had been raised to higher planes of life by
the incarnation and had been gifted by the Spirit
with preternatural insight and clearness of understanding in the things of God. The time had
come when God would trust men, even with his
own work.

In the same way the letter of Scripture was left
subject to the vicissitudes of time and history,
guarded only by the fidelity of the Church to the
sacred deposit. The result has been seen in the
late effort at revision of the text by patient, careful, scholarly men with all known manuscripts
and versions of the world before them. The
most diligent, long-continued search for errors,
omissions, and interpolations has brought to light
nothing that affects the great facts of the gospel
or the doctrines that have formed the substance of
the Church's faith and teaching from the beginning. The hate and persecutions, the clamors
and controversies of the ages have failed to do
serious damage to even the letter of the sacred
text. What criticism may yet do it is vain to inquire. It has its rightful province, and ought to
use all its resources to detect error and insure exact truth in the letter and substance of the record.
We have no reason to fear the result of any legitimate investigation. On the contrary, we should

insist that the Church itself, restrained and guided by the Holy Spirit, shall exhaust the resources of honest scholarship in the labor of perfecting the text and putting every fact of Scripture in its true light and just proportions. To refuse inquiry would be to dishonor the faculties and agencies which the Son of God chose and charged with this function and in no small degree to discredit the testimonies so borne to the world. The endowment of the day of Pentecost involved the right and power to use the ordinary means of human intercourse and, by necessary implication, the methods by which these shall be made as perfect as the conditions of this world will permit, while it furnished ample guarantee to true faith for the perpetuity and integrity of the word of God.

It is a subsidiary function of the Church to search out and provide for the publication of the proofs of Christianity on the human and earthly side. The stress of Christian appeal must, in the nature of the case, be laid upon the supernatural, the divine attestation and authority given to the gospel; and upon this, in the last issue, faith must be established. But it cannot be presumed that any real contradiction lies between the Word of God and the records of nature and history. These last are

his own work, marred though they may be by
human passion and misinterpreted by the preju-
dice, ignorance, and malice of men; and it is no
small part of the business of the Church of God
to set them in their true light and make manifest
the absolute agreement between the revelation
that God has made of himself in his Son and the
discoveries made of him from the things that are
made. It was a true spiritual impulsion that set
the Church, so soon as the faith itself was delivered, upon collecting and collating the evidences
of Christianity. It is our right to bring the whole
realm of nature into the kingdom of God, to lay
under contribution to the cause of Christ the historic and scientific wealth of the nations, and to
make the reason of the world subservient to the
interests of the gospel, " bringing into captivity
every thought," every process of reasoning, " to
the obedience of Christ."

3. The witness to Christ is borne in the order
and administration of the Church. The substance
of these is clearly indicated in the life and teachings of our Lord and in apostolic example and
instruction: the form of them is committed to
the care of the Church, which, under the direction of the same Spirit, adjusts them to the varying conditions of time and place as may best se-

16

cure the maintenance of the truth and the interests of men. Uniformity is no more necessary to the integrity of the Church of God than it is to the unity of nature or of the human race. The freedom of the Spirit is unmistakably affirmed as against the prescriptions and restrictions of the " law of carnal commandment." But the freedom of the Spirit is not lawlessness. The principle of authority is asserted with equal force, and the right and power are vested in the Church to maintain subordination to the truth and fidelity to moral obligation. Everywhere and always the living Church has had its pastoral and punitive discipline, for instruction, regulation of life, admonition, censure, and in extreme cases excommunication. "I know thy works, . . . and how thou canst not bear them which are evil" is the note of a true Church which the Lord himself gives.

It is an essential part of this function of the Church to provide for and maintain public worship and the administration of the sacraments. This is the opening confession and avowal of the faith before men, its provision for the edification and comfort of believers and for their fellowship in Christ, and is also the open way into the communion of saints for all who truly repent and are prepared to make confession of Christ and assume the obligations of Christian life. In vital relation to public worship is the provision which the Church is bound to make for the preaching of the gospel. According to divine appointment the great results sought are to be reached through this agency. It is through the apostolic word, the gospel preached with the Holy Ghost sent down from heaven, that men are to believe. Men of apostolic quality must be found for a work of such high import and imperative need, men who may give themselves to the word of God and prayer. To commit it to the accidents of natural endowment, to allow its degeneracy to the level of the platform or the hustings, or to reduce it to mere ethical instruction, is fatal to its significance and effect. The preaching of the gospel is the point where the divine power exhibits itself directly through the human utterance. Men hear the voice of God in the word of the divinely called and duly certified preacher. It may be doubted whether there is full recognition of the place and power of this ministry in the Church and of the extent to which it ought to be carried. The readiness with which the authority is conferred with insufficient inquiry into the higher qualities essential to the work and the indifference to the hearing of the word seem to mark a decline in the estimate of this branch of service that is unfavor-able to the aggressive movement of the Church.

Besides these things, it is a true part of the Church's ministry to organize efforts to do good to the bodies and the souls of men. Here, as in individual Christian life, the aim must be to repro-duce the ideal offered in our Lord's life. Heal-ing and teaching were combined in his service. The want and suffering, the ignorance and super-stition of the world make the same appeal to him now as in the days of his flesh. It cannot be doubted that if he were now on earth, with the vast resources of the Church of to-day at com-mand, he would send forth men, as he sent the seventy, through the length and breadth of this and all lands, to heal the sick, cleanse the lepers, cast out devils—to "heal all that are oppressed of the devil." He charged his disciples to do the works that he was doing, and promised that they should do even greater works than these. In its feeble and halting charities, missions, and educational movements the Church gives proof that the echo of the Lord's words is still sounding in its ears. But the sense of obligation is neither universal nor strong; and until a more enlightened and thor-oughly awakened conscience shall respond to the demand of the Son of God, the opportunities of the time will be wasted and the crying needs of the world remain unsatisfied.

4. One characteristic of the life of the Church as the witness for Christ remains to be noted: that which pertains to its relations to the secular life and power. It has been difficult, at some periods, to define accurately these relations, and determine the measure of rightful interference in the world's affairs. The individual member of the Church is also a member of the body politic, and cannot with a good conscience evade its responsibilities or refuse its duties. The rule for him is plain and simple and, to a true and bold adherent to his Lord, never difficult of application. In business, social, and civil affairs the principle holds good: "Whether ye eat, or drink, or whatsoever ye do, do all to the glory of God."

As a community the Church is segregated. It is in the world, but not of it. Within its own sphere it is bound to guard the life of the community from the intrusion of worldly elements and principles and suffer nothing that is in conflict with its one purpose and charge, to make Christ and his salvation known to men. It is quite within the province of the Church to exact of its members that in the discharge of their functions as citizens, in the conduct of business, in the regulation of the family, and in the observance of social requirements they shall conform to and illustrate the law of life given in and by the Son of Man.

The assertion and enforcement of these principles within the limits of its own life and action are indeed the Church's witness to the truth before the world. We cannot hope by projecting the Church as a secular force into the midst of the affairs of government and society to change the currents of human life. Degeneracy of spiritual quality and loss of true power must be the only results of such interference. The bold and uncompromising enunciation of every ethical and spiritual principle of the gospel, the due and guarded enforcement thereof within the body, and entire freedom from entanglement in worldly schemes, however fair and promising they may appear, are the only assurance of safety for the Church and of efficiency in its measures for saving men.

This rapid and inadequate sketch of the meaning and form of the testimony given by the Church is sufficient to put it in line with the foregoing witnesses and establish it upon the same ground as the medium of conveyance of divine revelation, the depository of divine power and representing in its individual and corporate character and work the life and working of the Son of God. It adds nothing to the testimony gone before save on the historic and earthly side. It has accumulated and stored up, as the centuries have gone by, the effects wrought by the gospel in human life and history for the ages to come. But it has challenged the world's faith in the Son of God, not upon the ground of these things, but because of the " demonstration of the Spirit and power " attendant upon its preaching and its ministries. If it has not lost its true quality, its presence and work in the world are a perpetual assertion of the immanence of God in the history of men, of the supremacy of Jesus Christ in every realm of being, and of the indwelling of the Spirit of God in the heart of every believer and in his body, the Church. Its power is divine; its grace is supernatural. It does not commit itself to the fortunes of the world; it does not intrust its work to natural agencies. Whatever may be its visible relations to this world, it has deeper, truer, more vital connections with the invisible and eternal world. In the last time it will be seen, not emerging from the darkness and chaos of time, but descending from God out of heaven. Its life, as that of each member, is hid with Christ in God, and thence it shall appear with him in glory.

And " every creature which is in heaven, and

on the earth, and under the earth, and such as are in the sea, and all that are in them, heard I saying, Blessing, and honor, and glory, and power, be unto him that sitteth upon the throne, and unto the Lamb forever and ever.''

> Let ev'ry kindred, ev'ry tribe,
>   On this terrestrial ball,
> To him all majesty ascribe,
>   And crown him Lord of all.

Lightning Source UK Ltd.
Milton Keynes UK
UKHW010612120219
337137UK00007B/1405/P